My Walk With Jesus

A Life Of Miracles

by Roy Smart

Index

Version 3. December 2020.

Foreword

The many times that I have NOT written a foreword for books hardly prepares me for writing this, my first. But I can honestly say that it gives me great pleasure so to do because it is about God and my life with Him and I feel, in connection with my stories, that God told me to write them all down. So here they are.

Since I became a Christian at the age of 38, at the time that my world fell apart, many years have passed and I am now in my 60's. This was the biggest change in my life and I have to tell you, it has been fantastic. I am thrilled that I have been able to tell you these few stories in this book. It will not be remarkable for it's literary style, but it is the simple truthfulness of this man who made a commitment to God that changed my life. Anyone who cares to read this book, Christian or not, will find it fascinating what may be done, if you put your trust in God.

Some names have been changed.

About The Author

For me life began on November 21st 1956. I was born in a little house: 9, Ryland Road, Kentish Town, London. Penultimate of five children: Evelyn, Linda, Terry, myself and Stephen.

Life for my Mum was hard looking after, feeding and clothing us on mostly on the £5 per week of Family Allowance. Her inner strength amazed me. She was constantly cleaning, ironing and washing, cooking, knitting and darning socks. Mum just did not stop.

Breathing problems hounded me during my early years. At the age of five I was taken to hospital. The doctor said that I was going to die, but Dad pushed for a second opinion. This second doctor said that as it was a cold winter day that all the windows open would help to cool my temperature of 105F. It worked.

Now that I have been a Christian for several decades I am able to look at those days before and recognise certain patterns. For example I recall that I was in the habit of calling upon God to save me from those perils that occasionally threaten all of us, such as car headlights cutting out on the darkest of roads, with promises of a life of my thanks to Him to follow. More than once a disaster was averted but I didn't follow through on my promises to the Almighty. Only once, on a holiday with my brother Stephen, did I thank God for what was happening, and I am glad that I did as on January 21st 1977 Stephen died. It turned my family upside down, but there was a small sliver of comfort for me that I had had that final holiday with my younger brother and that I had thanked God for it.

What follows now are a collection of stories of God's miraculous interventions in my life and of those around me and may not always be in chronological sequence. Each incident has a special place in my heart and encourages me about the love that God has for us all, if only we will let Him. The section headings are merely useful for identification of each story that has a beginning and an ending of its own. Each one is a reminder to me that God is above human limitations.

Roy Smart.   royandhisbook@gmail.com.   August 2020.

Out Of Body Experience

School, I would say, did not come easy for me, but you can only do your best. There are some things that stay in the memory; one for me was THAT swimming lesson at school. We were told to stand in a queue by the edge of the thirteen feet deep pool, that's the deep end, and jump in one by one. As I watched the queue diminish fear ran through my body. When it was my turn the instructor held a long pole towards me, told me to grip it and jump in. I wanted to shout "You know I can't swim!" but didn't. He pulled the pole around and in I went. Without even the slightest of pauses I was under the water. Not being able to swim coming up for air was not possible, and I found myself struggling panic and fear. Something happened under the water – I had an out of body experience. The part of me that came out was peaceful and calm as it watched the other part of me drown and was content to watch my, our, body die. The spirit that came out felt totally alive, much more alive than the earthly body ever felt. After that I recall nothing. Nothing about coming out the pool or who it was that pulled me out or whether I was presented to a doctor or if an ambulance was involved. I just don't know. All I know is that I was in the water and someone saved my life.

Girlfriend With Food Poisoning

My girlfriend Lynn and I went to Spain for a week. On the day of our return she was taken with food poisoning and the doctor was called. After his visit he told me that she was going nowhere and to find a certain medicine for her. I ran through the streets looking for a pharmacy and this was one of those pre-Christian moments of calling out to God for help with her healing. When I eventually found an open pharmacy I ran back to the hotel. But what did I find? She was up on her feet, dressed, packed and ready to go. In amazement I said "I thought you weren't well?" She answered "When the doctor was here I was terrible, but now am fine and the pain has gone." Selfishly I was more thankful for being able to take advantage of our tickets home than I was for the well-being of Lynn. I still had not learned that sometimes we fire up these little tiny prayers to God, not really expecting much, but God is a God of many surprises and I believe that He does it to draw our attention and to pull us to Him. He wants to help us in the good times and in the bad.

A Voice Says "He Is Looking For You"

The phone call was to tell me that my brother Stephen had died, though I didn't know it. My younger brother and I were inseparable so it was a call I needed to take. But in those days of landlines only, and me working on a roof deep within the building site, I wouldn't normally have known anything about it. I saw a young lad walking across the site away from me on my roof. Then a voice came from Heaven "Roy, he is looking for you". At the same moment this young lad span around on the spot and came marching straight to me. He climbed the ladder and said "Is your name Roy?" I ran to the office phone and it was my sister telling me to come home. A little thing to anyone else in the world, but this event meant the world to me.

The upsets that we all must suffer in life and the death of those dear to us, God may use to draw us to Him. At those times when my brother and later my Dad died I found myself asking questions about life: What does it mean? Why are we here? These questions helped me to understand that there is more to life than can be seen. Later I was ready to undertake a commitment to God and now understand that we need to be ready.

Dreams: My Marriage And A Car

My wife-to-be, Amanda, and I met shortly after the loss of my Dad. I had an unsettling dream in which my car went faster and faster; the brakes did not work and the car would not stop. The next thing I was standing at the roadside watching the car accelerating away from me towards a wall that it hit, but noiselessly. After waking I did not have a clue if the dream had any meaning and certainly hoped that not all dreams come true.

Eleven months later saw Amanda and I married and I took in her two children Paul and Verity. After a couple of years our own daughter Rachel was born to us.

A Little Old Lady Told Me That I Would Move To The Sea And Find Work

During a dry spell of work I was at home in the day when an elderly lady knocked on the door selling lace. Even though I did not have much money I found enough to buy a small piece of lace. She looked at me and said "You will find work and you will move down by the sea."

A Move To The Sea And Finding Work

Sure enough both of these happened within a couple of months where we found a house and I had an offer of work.

John The Christian

On the new building site I had a friend called John who gave me some audio tapes about pyramid selling. John was sure that this was his key to untold riches. He even went to worship with his wife, convinced that weak-minded Christians were sure to fall for the scam. Sadly not only were the Christians not that gullible but John was disconcerted by all the smiling faces and thought that perhaps he had been set up. The sermon started and John started preparing difficult questions in his mind ready for an argument after the service. But immediately that each question was formed within him the preacher would somehow know and answer each question there and then. This certainly gave John something to think about it.

It was the sort of Christian gathering wherein people are asked to come forward to give their lives to Christ. John was alarmed to find that he could not move until the whole evening was over. When he arrived home his prescient wife looked at him and said "You wanted to give your life to Jesus, didn't you?" John admitted this.

The next week the two of them attended at the same place and at that time John was able to answer the call and he gave his life to God. He never did sell his pyramid schemes to Christians and the next time I saw him he wasn't talking about get-rich-quick schemes, but about Jesus. This is before my own conversion and frankly I thought him a crazy, religious nutter, though John is still my friend and it was me that was far from the truth.

Adventures On The M5

When the job came to an end we said goodbye. Returning home from the job my car barely made it to my village before breaking down and needing to be towed by my friend Brian. He diagnosed a dead engine and the need for a new one. Being freshly out of work I did not have the large amount of money required for a new engine. I made Brian tow it for miles trying to bump start it - nothing would work. A builder needs a vehicle and this was a low point for me, I couldn't afford to fix it or to replace it. Deep in thought I looked up at the blue summer sky and said "God, if ever I need you, it's now." Brian, ever the optimist, said "Roy, try it just one more" so I put my hand through the window and turned the key and what do you know? It started. Brian and I agreed that neither of us could believe it. This broken down vehicle ran for another two years on the power of God alone and served as a daily reminder of the time that I relied on Him, though it took me a lot longer to put all the pieces of the puzzle into place.

Job Offer On The Phone

On the same day Brian said to me "Now the car is working, all you need to complete this is for someone to ring up to give you work". I certainly smiled at that. However the next day a carpentry contractor phoned with an offer, providing that I come over and prove myself. Naturally I popped over and did the tests: hanging some doors and then giving a house a second fix. It quite caught my ear the phrasing that he used next. He said "You never know, this site could be a blessing to you".

This site was ten minutes from home and the job lasted five years. Not only was the whole deal taking care of material needs but in time it was on that site that I came to know Jesus in His capacity of Saviour.

Both Arms In Pain

Shortly after starting this new job a pain started in my arms. This affected me at work and eventually by the end of the day I would be in bed with totally numb arms. I tried many suggested solutions but nothing would bring back the feeling and the numbness went on for three months. Then one day I surprised myself. My sister Linda was on the phone and I told her about my arms. She said "You better go to the doctor." A perfectly reasonable thing to say, but I surprised myself by replying "No, I am going to pray. If God is up there He is going to heal me."

Well, I remember saying a simple prayer, not really knowing what to say. That night I had a great night's sleep and I woke up pain free. What's more my arms have never hurt again. In hindsight God had His eye on me and maybe even prompted me to pray because that was not normal to me. I am pleased that at the time, the first time I displayed any basic faith in God, it proved a lesson for the rest of my life. Since then I have learned that where you put your last word is where you put your faith. What I mean by this is that when you have exhausted all your other options and hopes and they have not helped; the last place to which you turn for help, that is the thing in which you have faith. So when we have tried to fix it ourselves, when friends and family have failed to help, when we finally cry to God because we have nothing left – that is finally faith.

Lotto Numbers – Hope For A Fool

At one time I was coming home and again money was tight. I started thinking about the Lotto. Six numbers popped into my head with such force that I stopped the van to write them down and I told myself that I was going to play the Lotto and win. So sure and proud was I in my belief that I told a lot friends, but of course did not tell them the numbers. At this time home was a three bedroomed bungalow beside the sea and in it I told Amanda, but in those days she did not seem to listen to me.

I spent £1 each week to play my six special numbers. One week I missed buying a ticket when three of my numbers came up and was angry at losing my prize of £10. Of course I continued to play for many weeks to come. At the end of one week I was in the bath when my step-son Paul knocked on the door and said "Dad, have you heard the Lotto numbers?" I said "No, not really as I forgot to buy a ticket this week." But the TV in the lounge was loud enough to be heard in the bathroom, there were four of my numbers – I would have won a lot. I could not believe it – I had been certain that my numbers would come up but on the occasions that they did I had forgotten to buy a ticket.

For months more I kept buying the tickets without any wins until one day it finally occurred to me the lesson that God wanted me to learn. We cannot trust in luck or our "certain" numbers or some system. God wanted me to not trust in the Lotto and stop spending huge amounts of money by making me forget to buy a ticket and letting my numbers come up. Having blocked my false hope I should learn to trust in Him.

"The End Of All"

The next day I told my wife Amanda about it but all she could do was laugh. A few days later I went to see my Mum and the family. Talking with sister Evelyn, I said "Eve, I'm going to start to read the Bible." Eve said "If you are going to read the Bible, I am going to buy one for you." When back at home Amanda said "If you start reading that, it will be the end – the end of all!" It seemed like an odd thing to say, but she turned out to be absolutely right.   Amanda did not like me reading the Bible so to make her happy I told her I would stop. But what she wanted me to do, and how I wanted to make her happy could not oppose God who, in His Grace and mercy, was slowly drawing me to Him. Every time Amanda settled down to read her magazines I would pop upstairs and read the Bible; I felt that reading about what Jesus had done for us was in some way feeding me – like a spiritual nourishment. I was thinking "If this is all real, then I owe God everything. If Jesus Christ is God and died for us then there is no sacrifice too great for me to make for Him." That was a thought heavy and always present in my mind as I read.

I am so glad that God drew me to Him and did not allow me to push Him away or let me turn to the side because all of the things that He subsequently led me through or let me experience or witness happening turned out to be the best journey of my life.

On the way home from work one day I called in to see a friend about a little job he was offering. Just as I was leaving he asked "Roy, what would you do if your marriage broke up?" I looked straight into his eyes and said "I would most probably turn to God." It did not appear to me to be a strange question because he was having problems in his marriage and needed help and advice. On more than one occasion Saul would ring up to speak with Amanda, sometimes even 10 or 11 o'clock in the evening wanting someone to come over to speak with him. Trusting Amanda fully I often said "You go to see him as I have work in the morning."

One day I was working and a feeling came that I should go home at midday. At home there was no sign of Amanda. When she came home I asked how her day was. As she did not answer I felt that there was something wrong.

Soon after this I came home from work in the evening and Amanda said "I want a divorce and you to leave right now. To save any argument I did go but first I said goodnight to the children and then I left.

That evening I drove around for a while, not knowing what to do. After a little while I headed back into town to a car park that I knew, and there I slept in the van for three nights. Those winter nights were long and hard and cold, reflecting my wife as my marriage came to an end. How we change. Upon reflection I remembered the dream mentioned above in **Dreams: My Marriage And A Car**. I hadn't known where the dream came from; God, the evil one or my imagination, so I hadn't paid attention to it and the dream had been forgotten. Suddenly it is ten years later and I am thinking about the dream that had become real and alive. Finally the realisation arrived and I understood what it meant. This had been the dream: I was driving down the road in my car. The car put on speed and even though I applied the brakes they did not work and the car went faster and faster. Suddenly I was on the side of the road watching the car from the outside as it went straight into a brick wall. There was no noise or explosion or mess, the car just vanished.

The interpretation was this: When I met Amanda I had my own house and sports car. I took great care of it and was quite possessive. In some ways Amanda took the place of that car when I married her and I took great care of her and tried to be supportive. Towards the end of the marriage she was pushing for a divorce. After this declaration I was no longer in the marriage, I was standing outside watching it accelerate towards the inevitable brick wall of divorce court. Here there was no mess as I was already learning to rely on God. We will come to more of this later as you journey with me from unbelief to belief.

After sleeping in the van for three nights and working in the day I needed a shower. A friend at work came over and said "Roy, are you going home?" I said "No, my wife has kicked me out." He said "Do you pay the mortgage?" I said "Yes." "So how can she kick you out?" I agreed that this was a good point. I rang Amanda and told her that I needed a wash and change of clothes. She agreed but informed me that I needed to be out by the time the children arrived home from school. As soon as I entered the house the phone rang, it was my friend Barry who said "Roy, whatever you do don't leave the house." Then he rang off. Straight away the phone rang again and it was my brother Terry. He said "Whatever you do, don't leave the house. If she wants to leave and end the marriage let her, but you stay in the house." After a shower I rang Amanda and told her my new thoughts about staying in the house. She was not happy and accused me of making the children homeless. I replied "I am not making them homeless and I am happy for them and you to live here. We could try again." Well, she moved out and at first would not let me see the children, which was hard on me. As time went on only Rachel, our daughter, came to see me and Verity and Paul, Amanda's from her previous marriage did not come. That first weekend was hard and I remind myself of its importance to me.

Daughter Rachel Aged Seven

When Rachel was only seven it was a beautiful August day and some friends in the town invited us over for a barbecue. Rachel was excited by the prospect. I said that first Flopsy the Dogsy needed a comfort call in the back garden, a lovely dog but something of a rascal. Flopsy found the side gate open and made a mad dash for it. Rachel was very upset that he had gone. I said "Don't be sad, he will come back." "Oh Daddy, will Flopsy come back?" I said "Yes" as I knew it to be true, it wasn't the first time that he had gone walkabout, but sometimes it would be three to four days before he used up all activities to be found and would wander home. Sometimes the dog-catcher would bring him back. We looked for Flopsy but with no success. We decided to leave the side gate open for when the dog came home.

We set off to walk to our friend's house for the barbecue. Rachel was lagging behind and I encouraged her to walk a little faster. She said "I am just doing a prayer to Jesus for Flopsy to come home." I said that that was really nice of her, and that Flopsy is sure to come home now.

We had a lovely time at the barbecue, four hours with good friends. Then Rachel and I walked home as the sun set over the sea showing us lovely colours and creating a special moment. Rachel was very tired so I carried her and as she was close to sleep in my arms she opened her eyes and said "Daddy, does Jesus speak to you?" This was a total surprise and I said "Yes, if you listen. Darling, why did you ask that?" She said "Because Jesus has spoken to me and told me that Flopsy is fine and he will be home in a couple of minutes." We had just arrived home and I turned the key in the lock, and then into the kitchen for a cup of tea. Suddenly the side gate slammed shut. I ran out into the garden then through the gate into the road but there was nothing at all to be seen. I came back into the garden noting that the side gate was shut, but there was Flopsy in the garden behind the shut gate. I was amazed as from the time my daughter said that he would be home in a couple of minutes to seeing him was indeed how long it was. Truly, truly a miracle. God had spoken to my daughter about something so trivial for anyone else, but of the utmost importance to her.

Unexpected Directions

On the way back from visiting my Mum Rachel and I stopped for some fast food and an ice cream sundae. Back in the car Rachel said that she didn't want the sundae and put it on the rear parcel shelf for me to have later, then she reminded me to ring her when I arrived home.

After dropping her off with her mother I noticed the sundae in the rear view mirror and stopped for a little snack. Eating whilst driving would have been a bad move and made me think about accidents. As I set off I was cautious and still thinking about accidents. Having driven through the tiny country roads for ten minutes I reached a staggered junction and an ambulance streaked right in front of me. In the direction in which I was about to go there was an accident and traffic was stationary so I went across the road looking for an alternative route.

Very soon I was completely lost so I appealed to God for directions. Rounding a corner there was a cottage on the left and an elderly lady leaning out of the window waving me down. She told me that there had been an accident and cars are being diverted onto the country lanes. But how could she possibly know? Then she provided me with directions and promptly shut the window without waiting for my thanks.

On the evening phone call I recounted all this to my daughter who professed amazement.

Pain In My Head

Each night I would read a portion of the Bible before sleep and I see it now, but not then, that God was drawing me in. About a week later I had a headache for three days and felt quite rough. At work in the late afternoon one co-worker friend said "I am going home, are you?" I said yes, but did not have anyone to whom to go home. On the way home I asked myself whether the headache was something that I could pray about, after all there are worse problems in the world. It seemed to me that I shouldn't. Upon reflection I think that it was because I was frightened that God would not answer my prayer. That realisation made me think "You know, I think I will ask God to remove this pain in my head." It was a simple prayer with no big words, asked in Jesus' name. Instantly the pain went. Arriving home I rang my Mum and family to tell them all about it.

God Calls: "Make A Choice"

Looking back on my life God had revealed Himself to me in that life and also through my daughter and it was perhaps time that I formally did something about it. One day soon after I came home to the bungalow and there was an all-pervasive smell of flowers. Although the aroma was so strong there was not one flower in the house. Then there was a loud distinct voice that said "Hey Roy, you need Jesus in your life." It was totally amazing, here am I, in my house all alone, or at least I had thought that I was alone, and hearing this loud voice telling me what I need. It was the biggest wake up call of my life – I had met God and had seen and felt His hand upon my life and it was time for me now to make the choice: follow self or follow God.

Many years later I found out that many saints from history said that the presence of a strong sweet smell but with no obvious cause usually indicates the presence of the Holy Spirit.

That night all the children came to visit: Verity, Paul and Rachel. It was great to see them after about two weeks of being alone. When it was time to leave the children did not want to go and said that they wanted to stay with Dad, but Amanda would not allow it. Emotions were high as Amanda ushered them out of the door and my temper flared and when I hit the door I broke my fist.

Amanda came back to see what had happened, and kindly took me to the hospital. That night the doctors operated on my hand and I was in hospital for three days. I was sent home with hand and arm in plaster making life alone a little tricky. I had twelve weeks of work and otherwise no money. Not knowing what else to do I started to play the Lotto again once more in hopes of the big win. After a few weeks of no reward I stopped doing it and was sitting in the lounge one Sunday morning flicking through Teletext and happened on the Lotto numbers. Amazingly I had five numbers but once again had not bought a ticket, upon which I would have won a couple of thousand of pounds – very useful in straightened times.

Suddenly A Christian

One evening I was putting the pieces together and thinking about all the times that my numbers had come up but that they were always on weeks that I forgot to buy a ticket. I was fed up about it and staring around the walls I thought "Even these walls cannot help me." I felt lost with no direction like being in a long dark tunnel with no light at the end to guide me onwards.

Then I thought about the words of the time when I was alone in the house "You need Jesus in your life." and I had read some of the Bible and I thought "Yes, I do need Jesus in my life." I was seated in my lounge and, feeling bad about them, repented of my sins by saying sorry for all the terrible things that I have done. After all the things that had happened, all the prompts, all the times that I had nearly got it, I finally did it and asked Jesus into my life. I felt the presence of God enter into my home, I no longer felt alone or hopeless as His presence wrapped around me and His peace overwhelmed me. I knew that this was the beginning of something new – the phrase "born again" seemed entirely appropriate. God's Spirit was palpably upon me, the seed of Eternal Life had been planted within me. I broke down in tears.

First Time To Worship, The Sermon Ends My Marriage

The next day was Sunday so I wandered into a Christian gathering for the first time. Just to amaze me further the pastor based his sermon on the break up of marriages. Afterwards I rang my family and told them all about the events of the last couple of days, but they didn't have much of a response for me and I had rather expected something more. I rang brother-in-law Mike as he and his wife Eve, my sister, were the only Christians in the family at that time. He was more supportive and said "Roy, it's a great journey." With my world falling apart around me my last chance of hope was in God and I felt that I had nothing to lose.

Bonus Ball

I had nothing to lose but everything to learn. Still having no money I didn't know what to do so I decided to find my old Lotto numbers. At that stage I believed that there was something special about them as they had come up and yielded big wins, though not to me. They had come up as wins on three, four and five numbers. Imagine if they came up with the sixth ball - the bonus ball? However the paper with the numbers on had gone from my bedroom drawer. This appeared to be the last chance of accruing extra money. Amanda had stopped all of our bank accounts and taken all the balances.

Tax Man

At last I did the right thing and asked God to help me, straight away a quiet voice in my head said "Roy, I am your bonus ball. When you have nothing in this world and all you have is God, then you have everything." How amazing. The next day in the post was a cheque for £1,500. It was an unexpected, unapplied for tax rebate from the tax man. This money provided very well until I was able to find more work. Praise God. It was the first time that I could see that having God as a plan and purpose in my life was worthwhile. Not as a means to gaining material riches, but as a means to learning humility and utterly depending upon Him. As you continue to read my little collection of stories sometimes you will feel challenged, sometimes you will be inspired by my walk with Jesus. We are all on a journey together and if we can encourage one another it helps us to grow stronger in our Christian faith and this helps us to be bolder for Jesus as we allow each day to be His and to live, not according to our own wants, but to ask God for guidance.

> "I am not ashamed of the Gospel, because
> it is the power of God for the salvation of
> everyone who believes."
> - Romans 1:16 KJV[1].

God Speaks Again, In The Divorce Room

As the weeks went on I was missing my children more and more. I was applying through the courts for custody, but unsure if

---

1   KJV = King James Version.

I was doing the right thing in the right way. I asked God if Rachel would be better off with me or with her Mum and Rachel's half-brother and half-sister. I thought back to the death of my brother Stephen and pulled out his records to play them. One was called *"You Tried To Warn Me"* by Piero Umiliani (1968). My Mum and Dad had never liked motorbikes and repeatedly warned Stephen of the danger. When I pulled out that record it had a big impact. God can speak to us in any way and grab your attention; He can surprise us and performs miracles. In my room was a box of around 200 records all mixed up and I also had the Bible open with me. I prayed "Father, I am going to open the Bible and ask for a sign over whether Rachel, my sweet little daughter, would prefer to live with me or her Mum." This was a very bold thing to do as treating the Bible like Lotto by plucking out verses at random, and hoping to come up trumps, is a dangerous practice and can be a way deluding ourselves. I was still new to my Christian life and had so much to learn, and I was unguided with only my own blind gropings and God's mighty elbow of correction.

Despite all this I looked down at the Bible and this is what I read:

> *"Then they said 'Let us call the girl and ask her about it.' So they called [Rachel] and asked her: 'Will you go with this man?' 'I will go.' she said.*
>
> — Genesis 24:57 LXX[2].

At reading this I wept and wept. I felt that God would, in His own time, restore Rachel to me and restore the time lost between us. The divorce in general and the custody of the children could become messy if I continued to fight for them through the courts. What sort of solution to the problem would Christ have offered me if I asked Him? Still a junior Christian and being unaware of the risks I thought of the message that I had extracted from the title of the one in my brother's collection *"You Tried To Warn Me"*. I wondered if the same thing would work again. So I told God my idea and went to pluck out a random record that would dictate to me whether or not I should continue to fight for my child to live

---

2   LXX = Septuagint. The Christian Old Testament.

with me. The first record to be pulled out was *"Put Yourself In My Place"* by the Isley Brothers. I prayed "Lord, I don't know what this means. Can I try again so that you can speak to me?" So I plunged my hand into the box of about 200 records and pulled out *"Everything Is Going To Be Alright"* by Bob Marley. I understood this to be a sign to not fight the court case that was due in a few days. It felt right to me that if God wanted my daughter to live with me, then He would make it happen without me making a big fuss over it. Amen and so be it.

Two weeks later I was in the waiting room at court with four other people. Amanda walked in and my heart started racing and I was thinking "Don't sit next to me, there are plenty of other spare seats." Then there was that loud clear voice inside me that said "Roy, Roy. Do not worry for the greater one is in you than is in the world". Suddenly peace wrapped around me, my heart rate returned to normal. Praise the Lord. This put a smile on my face and I started to laugh. Amanda and the others in that waiting room must have thought me strange. But I simply knew that God was in control and He would look after those who look to Him, as I was learning how. God would look after me. At this point I was 38 as a man, but a mere baby as a Christian and did not have a good knowledge of the Bible. It was much later that I found out that what that voice had said to me was a quote:

> You are of God, little children, and have overcome them: because greater is He that is in you, than he that is in the world.
> - 1 John 4:4 KJV.

I have learned from experience that God will always confirm in the Bible and bring it to fulfilment. As I tell you more stories you will see this time and time again as God showed His will to me in dreams, in prayer, in the Bible whilst talking with God and waiting on His will. It must always be in God's timing and not according to your own strength or abilities. I serve the Greatest Boss in the universe and He wants to be close to each one of the children that He created. I pray that this book will be one of many means that God uses to bring you closer to Him.

Rachel Calls Confirming A Bible Reading

Two months later Rachel called me from her Mum's house in the village. She said "Dad, I want to come and live with you." "Darling, what has brought this on?" It brought to mind the Bible verse from that night with my brother's records:

"I will go." she said.

I asked to speak to her Mum whilst thinking "if Amanda says yes now then that proves that the matter was under God's control." We were still fighting the divorce. "What's this about Rachel wanting to come and live with me?" "Yes, she has been saying for the last two months." It was about two months since that Bible verse. "Amanda, how do you feel about it?" "It's fine with me if that's what she wants." I replied "OK, you know that I am having Rachel for half term week, if she says any more during that time she can stay here." However during that week Rachel did not say anymore, this was difficult and confusing for me and I left the matter to see what developed. It is hard times like these that God can use to build us up and make us stronger. The problem is that sometimes we miss these lessons as our heart is set on our own ambitions and we wallow in self-pity. "Draw near to God and He will draw near to you."

My Baptism

Coming to the end of my twelve weeks off because of the broken hand and ready for work, I was learning to trust in God and felt hungry for more, and was telling everyone I could about the Gospel. The day that I returned to work the boss asked if I knew a good roofer. I told him about my friend John, we gave him a ring and he started on Monday, straight out of one job and into this one with no days lost. This was the John that I had called a religious nutter, how wrong was I? Now there were two Christians on site working alongside each other, praising God, spreading the Gospel and encouraging each other.

John invited me to a Christian venue with him in Chippenham. That night I was not feeling too good as there was a pain in my chest. It was one of those healing services and there seemed to be several people benefiting from it and being healed of all sorts of things. So I asked God in the name of Jesus to heal the pain in

My Walk With Jesus

my chest and, praise Him, the pain went away. God's power was working within me. We talked about it all the way home.

John asked me if I had been baptised, he told me it was a public declaration and represents the death, burial and resurrection of Jesus Christ and as He was raised from the dead we also will be raised from the dead. At that time I was attending the Church of England, but they do not baptise anyone, they only Chrismate[3] babies. Sometime later my friend Bobby invited me to the place that he attended, so I went to have a look. It was an Evangelical group and very lively and so totally different from the last place, additionally they baptise. I attended regularly and some weeks later confessed my faith and was baptised in the name of the Father, the Son and the Holy Spirit. When my two friends put me under the water I felt something happen to me. As I came out of the water I felt like a completely different man. My arms went straight up into the air to praise Jesus. I was doubly thrilled as all three of my children came to watch. What a great day all round. I also stood up to give some testimonies to the audience. A testimony is a story of a miracle by God. All of these stories in this book are testimonies. I talked about the time Rachel had said God has spoken to her about Flopsy coming home in a couple of minutes and how that had made me think. The second story was when I had two encounters personally with God; the first that time when the house was filled with the smell of flowers and the next that time when my world was falling apart but God seemed to be always with me and so I decided to give myself to God and His presence was all around me. After this the band played my chosen song "There Is None Like You" by Lenny LeBlanc.

Praying Aloud

Soon it was half term week and all three lovely children were staying with me: Verity, Paul and Rachel. We had a great week. Rachel didn't say anymore about living with me, so I didn't raise it either. When I took them all back to their mother's house she didn't say much, just told the children to come in and shut the door. This was upsetting after the children having a great week. Back at my bungalow I went into the dormer bedroom to have a read of the Bible. Sitting on the bed I opened up the Bible, then I

---

3   Chrismation is anointing with water. Baptism is complete immersion.

thought "No, I will pray first", so I put it down and knelt on the floor. As I prayed I felt that I wasn't so much in the bedroom as more importantly with God. As I relaxed into this these beautiful words came to me and I spoke them aloud for God. Even though it was in English it somehow felt much more beautiful and as if no words in our language could approach them. Two words were repeated over the top "Listen, listen" and as I continued reciting these words all of a sudden I switched into tongues – often described as the language of the angels – and it felt like the right thing to do. I tried to switch back to English but each time I just flipped back to tongues. After about forty minutes of prayer I arose from my knees and thought about what had just happened. I had seen some of the Evangelicals do this and it seemed like a gift of God and also something worth having, but I had never thought that God would give me the gift. It seemed the right time to open the Bible and looking for it I found it open on the bed.

"Listen, listen."   - Isaiah 55:2 LXX.

This, for me, was total confirmation and as I have said before, if it's of God He will always confirm it, in one way or another. What is impossible for man is possible for God.

Paul's Face Glowed And The Pain Was Gone

On one occasion Paul my step-son came to stay with me for the weekend. As I said goodnight to him he said that he had a very bad pain in his stomach and he asked me for something for it. I went to have a look in the kitchen for something suitable, but could not find anything so I went back to Paul. His face was glowing, I said "Paul, are you alright?" He said "Yes, Dad, I am fine. When you were in the kitchen I said a prayer and the pain instantly went away." I replied "Praise God" but inside I felt like I had let God down by going to look for medicine and hadn't first asked God for healing for Paul. You know what? Wherever you put your last word is where you put your faith and at that point I put it in medicine and not in God. But by Paul praying for himself hopefully it strengthened his faith. I took Paul's hand and asked for forgiveness and thanked God that He had healed Paul. Returning to his mother Paul told her what had happened but I don't think that she believed him.

"And it came to pass, when Moses came down from mount Sinai with the two tables of testimony in Moses' hand, when he came down from the mount, that Moses knew not that the skin of his face shone while he talked with Him. And when Aaron and all the children of Israel saw Moses, behold, the skin of his face shone; and they were afraid to come nigh him."

- Exodus 34:29-30 KJV.

God Suggests That I Sell My House

Weeks later Amanda told me that she was moving to the Cotswolds, which I was not happy about. For the regular visits to the children it would mean driving eighty miles each way. I asked myself if I wanted to move to keep close to the children and prayed about it for a month. After the divorce I had a big mortgage on the bungalow, this could be a good opportunity to reduce that.

Going to worship one Sunday morning I had a gut feeling that I would receive my answer there. Unfortunately I had forgotten that it was the day when they changed their service time from 11:00 to 10:30. Arriving at 10:45 I was pleased with being early and entered to find everyone there and the service under way, with only one free chair in the back row. As soon as I was seated Davies Harris the pastor asked if anyone wanted to say a prayer or to thank God just to come forward and tell everyone about it. Immediately the question over selling the house came to me so I put my head down and said a silent prayer about it, like this: "Lord, there have to be about 200 people here today, I need an answer and I need it now about where You want me to live my life and what to do with the property that You have given to me. Should I sell? Should I rent it out? Should I take in lodgers?"

I opened my eyes to find that the woman next to me was Davies Harris' wife Jo. She went up to the stage and took a microphone. Although I recognised her we had not spoken and I knew nothing about her. The she spoke and it blew me away. She said "There is someone here who is concerned with the way their life is going and the property that they have. I am being told to tell that person, who ever it may be, to let it go and follow

God." Tears of joy were running down my face. I found it hard to reconcile the God who created everything in existence with Him who had tried and tried and tried to grab my attention before I came to faith and the way that He blesses me, though I don't deserve it. As I give back to Him in service so I must become less so that Jesus may become greater. If I am to become the likeness of Jesus I cannot be deflected in any way. When Jo came back to her seat I told her that the message was for me and about my prayer just before she said it. We hugged and praised God.

After the service I told everyone and at home rang brother-in-law Mike. He told me to test the matter. I was sure it was of God but agreed and felt that I had nothing to lose. The next Sunday I said the same prayer and another lady, Janet Brown, was on the stage. She said that she had been told that there was someone present who felt like they were hanging off a cliff edge by a rope and were frightened to let go. But God is saying "I will catch you". God is amazing, how does He do it? I love Him and I am never going to let Him go. You see, the honest problem was that I loved my little bungalow overlooking the sea. Plus it had been the family home and was still somewhere familiar for the children to come. Amanda knew that I loved having the children but she also seemed to like to make it hard for me.

One morning I was ready to step out of the door to work at 8:00 when Amanda arrived with the children for me to look after because she was going out and she just left. All four of us were all seated in the parlour and I was wondering what to do. As a contractor I was not in a position to take days off as it would mean no pay and possible loss of the contract. I asked God to help me concerning this and as soon as I had finished praying the phone rang. It was my friend Tracey up the road and the very first thing she said was "Roy, do you have your children with you today? Yes? Fine, I will come and get them and they can come here for the day." I had to praise the Lord, He is a God of surprises and wants to be a part of our lives. The Bible says:

"O taste and see that the Lord is good."
- Psalms 33:9 LXX.

Terry Takes Me To The Alpha Course

A new carpenter started on site called Terry. We became friends and without me saying anything he told me that he knew that I was a Christian, so I took this as an opening of a door and we talked about the Gospel. A couple of days later Terry rang to ask if I knew of rooms to rent for him and his girlfriend. I thought of these words of John the Baptist:

> *"He that has two coats, let him impart to him that has none; and he that has meat, let him do likewise."*
> - Luke 3:11 KJV.

As my bungalow had two spare bedrooms I offered him the use, short term only as it was going on the market as the Lord directed me. The next day Terry and Karen moved in. I was excited as I felt it right that God wanted them with me. Karen told me that her Mum is a Christian and had been praying for a Christian to take them in. I rang Karen's Mum and we had a great chat and became good friends.

The timing was good for me as I had agreed to help with the local Alpha Course for non-believers who want to know more about the Christian faith. Terry, Karen and I discussed it and they agreed to attend the Alpha Course. It was a twelve week course with food.

Karen was also looking for a job and was successful with the local Pontin's Holiday Camp. I returned home on a Tuesday night expecting Karen to be ready for the first evening of the course. It took me a moment to remember that she would be working late at her new job. I went upstairs to my bedroom rather confused and prayed "Lord, I don't understand what is going on. I believe with all of my heart that you have put this young couple under my roof so that they can hear the Gospel via the Alpha Course and all of a sudden it has all gone wrong." I was taking out my frustration on God because I did not understand. Downstairs the door slammed so I ran down. It was Karen, she said "I don't like the job and felt uncomfortable, so had to walk out." I laughed out loud and Karen asked why. I said "I was just upstairs having a go at God because your job stopped you coming on the course, then all of a sudden you come in and tell me you have just handed in your notice, now you can come on the course, because I believe that getting to know God is more important than any job."

That night we all went along and had a great time also meeting new friends. At the end we all said a little something about ourselves and, if a Christian, how we came to know Jesus. This guy Mike told his story and concluded with his present struggles with his weight and need to go to a gym and need for a partner. Well, muggins here piped up and volunteered to go with him. We became friends and brothers in Christ. After the gym we would undo our good work over a pint. On one occasion one drink turned into two as we discussed God, our usual topic of conversation. Mike leaned back in his chair and said "Do you know what, Roy? I really love the Lord." I looked him in the eye and said "Do you really?" His face started to puff up and turn red and he looked apologetic but continued "But do I love the Lord? Do I really love Him?" He went onto say that his reading of the Bible had slipped and so had his service to God because Jesus was not at the centre of his life. That's why he was coming to the Alpha Course to re-incentivise himself. I realised that we can deceive others, but we cannot deceive ourselves.

Dear Reader, may I ask you something, where do you stand in relation to God? Perhaps you, like me, will be challenged by these words.

> *"Man shall not live by bread alone, but by every word that proceedeth out of the mouth of God."*
>
> - Matthew 4:4 KJV.

And:

> *"He that overcometh, the same shall be clothed in white raiment; and I will not blot out his name out of the book of life, but I will confess his name before my Father, and before His angels."*
>
> - Revelation 3:5 KJV.

After our chat Mike started to tidy up his relationship with God and we even started our own prayer group in his little flat. On one occasion we had taken it upon ourselves to go into the street to preach the Gospel and we were having a pray about it. Mike said "When we are out on the street and we meet someone in a wheelchair, have we enough faith to pray for their healing?" As I have said before, God always confirms and right as Mike asked me this testing question a Biblical verse popped up into my head.

"And they departed, and went through the towns, preaching the gospel, and healing everywhere."
- Luke 9:6 KJV.

I told this to Mike and that it appeared to me to be a backing to get on with it. Most of all to do what we feel is God-appointed work and that everything else would follow along. I went on "If we put God first He will bless us and as I go on with my testimonies you will see that with that step of faith and trust in God to do the work that Jesus has called us to do, that we can do it, because Jesus died on the cross and that after He ascended into Heaven that the Holy Spirit was sent into the world to aid people to turn to God, through Jesus Christ, and receive the Holy Spirit." I was trying to say that whether or not we are called upon to heal is irrelevant, what is important is to run to the position to which God calls us, and all other duties may then be addressed.

More Mikes, More Trouble

The next weekend I went down to Bedfordshire to see my family, I had intended to go with my brother-in-law, the other Mike, as he invited me to a prayer meeting in London as he played in the band, but decided not to go and instead spend time with my Mum and family, so Mike-in-law went on his own. At 9:30 on the Saturday morning he rang me up in a terrible state, he had left his guitar leads and amp at home. "There are 1,100 people due here in an hour and I've left the tools of my trade behind. Please can you bring it all down to the middle of London?" Well I didn't have a clue how to find him when suddenly in walked my brother Terry to see his Mum. I absolutely could not remember the last time he had been there but as soon as he had pushed his face around the door I jumped onto him crying "Help!" I told him the situation but Terry simply and calmly asked for the phone, rang Mike back, took directions and drew me a map. Fifteen minutes later in the car with my sister and all the gear we were hot trotting it to London, landmark of Euston Station at 10:20 and with Mike who plugged in and strummed his first chord at 10:30. That's worth a 'Praise God'.

Flopsy The Dogsy Runs Away

The next day I returned home with the other Terry and Karen still in residence. The atmosphere was a bit tense as Karen had a habit of leaving the door open and my dog would escape. Once I was just about to leave for work and Flopsy saw his chance and set off at top speed. I tried running after him but compared to his speed only provided him with a comedy incentive as his fur blew in the wind and he looked at me with his tongue flapping about. He was a lovely dog but loved his freedom and could be something of a rascal. He reached the end of the cul-de-sac and of the two exits presenting themselves to a happy dog, Flopsy took the executive decision of going between the two into the fields and I could only gaze at his escaping behind until he disappeared. Oh well, nothing I can do on foot, so I went back to the van and tried to head him off in the village. The part of the plan concerning the van and arriving in the village went fine, the part concerning waiting for Flopsy took a long time as there was no sign of him. Looking at the time yet again I decided enough was enough and that it was time to go to work.

There was a chance that someone would call out the dog-catcher, but that would result in a bill of £35 for me – about a half days wages. Well, why not pray about it? "Lord Jesus who created all things, please help me, please help Flopsy to come back quick as I have to go to work and I should like to avoid the dog-catcher's bill." God quickly proved that all things are under His watchful eye as His directions popped into my head "Go back." Of course I have agreed to obey things such as this by now but I said to God "I will go back, but would you show me these events through Your eyes, not mine?" Going back seemed wrong to my human mind because Flopsy had come this way, not that way. I saw two friends but they had not seen my dog. As we were talking it felt like a hand touched my shoulder and I turned around, but there was no-one there. However far away at the other end of the bay was a bouncing happy dot that rang a bell. I jumped in the van and drove to the end of the bay whereat

Flopsy was happy to climb into the van, adventure accomplished, happiness had, and mayhem caused.

Yes I had Flopsy back again, but the point is that God is trustworthy, praiseworthy and faithful and knows all things and hears our prayers when we cry out to Him. I think that this was the lesson learned about seeing through God's eyes. The point is not the dog, the point is to lean on God.

More M5 Adventures – The Broken Down Yellow Mini

The next week I went to see my sister in Bedfordshire again who had just had an operation on her back. It was one of those weekends where everything goes wrong. Clearly nature had a spare set of disasters and realised that they could all be spent in one go on me and my family. There was trouble with the van and I loaned the key to my brother-in-law Mike who broke off the key in the door lock. I borrowed a car, and that broke down. My nephew smashed up his Mum's car and nearly killed himself. It was quite the traumatic weekend but always nice to see the family.

On that dark November Sunday evening, I was going home to Weston-Super-Mare on the M4. I always liked the long journey as I could play religious tapes; talks and music or have time to pray. This night there seemed to be one car after another broken down on the hard shoulder of the motorway. I could not help them as it is against the law to stop on a motorway, they would have to use the emergency phones.

Conversationally I said to God "Why are there so many cars broken down tonight?" and as I was driving along not really thinking or doing much a picture of a yellow Mini flashed into my head. It was also broken down, had on it's flashing warning lights and it was an N registration. Into my head God spoke "That will be a long shot won't it?" I admitted that of all the different cars on the road, of all those that could be near here and then the subset of those that would be in trouble, it would be high random number that would foretell this one particular make, colour, age, lights flashing etc. For ten miles I carefully looked ahead as it seemed apparent to me that I was going to see that same car, even though all the other broken down cars had ceased.

Elijah the prophet believed that the rain was coming and told his servant:

"And he said to his lad, "Go up, and look the way of the sea." And the lad looked and said, "There is nothing." And Elijah said: "Now you - go again seven times." And the lad returned seven times. And it happened at the seventh time, and behold, a little cloud - like the sole of a person's foot - bringing water."

- 3 Reigns 18:43 LXX.

Elijah trusted in God, focused on what he knew was going to happen, and the rain came.

As I continued on the M4 then onto the M5 I was still looking for this little yellow Mini. Coming towards Nailsea there were road works and the motorway lost a lane and the traffic all slowed down. I was in the slow lane with no hard shoulder only a line of cones to the left. And then there it was, tucked behind the cones with it's hazard lights on, an N registration little yellow Mini. Once again I was not legally allowed to stop, and there seemed to be no one in it. So what was the point? Well why did Elisha, the servant of Elijah, have to go and look seven times? As with the return of Flopsy the dogsy it is not always the item right before your face that is the point, it is the underlying trust that you can have upon God that is the valuable part. God gave me an image and I trusted that I would see it and after something of a wait I was ready to see it. This was just a little training and practice for my relationship and trust in God.

"For what saith the scripture? Abraham believed God, and it was counted unto him for righteousness."

- Romans 4:3 KJV.

It is something of a humbling moment to realise that God has had His eye on you and you have just had some quality time with one's own Creator. So I drove on, emotionally overcome by the realisation that God had wished to have that special time with this unworthy servant and I was praising God for His condescension. Then the Holy Spirit rushed through me and I collapsed into tears of great joy that God had seen fit to be with me.

My Walk With Jesus

Selling Sandboy

The next weekend Terry and Karen went away and it was then that God told me that it was time to put my bungalow Sandboy in the village of Sandbay on the market, which I did. The estate agents did all the things that estate agents like to do and when looking around offered to put up a For Sale sign as it would speed up the sale. However I declined and explained that I was doing everything in God's timing and instruction and He has left signal that it will sell quick. It is always a good way to address your ego to be laughed at in the face, but he who laughs last is he whose bungalow sold in two days. The couple were only the second viewers and their offer went in on the same day. The six weeks of conveyancing were completely smooth. I gave in to a childish urge and went to the estate agents to see the woman who had laughed at me to try an "I told you so" but controlled myself so that it wasn't gloating, but it gave an opportunity to talk about faith in God.

Terry and Karen were told and that we had six to eight weeks to find our next homes. They kept asking if I had done the right thing and I explained about the events leading up to it and my conviction that it was at the prompting of God and my attempts to follow Him. In my own prayer time I brought up the matter with the Almighty and pointed out that without my own house I was now free and could go anywhere, whether I like it or not, and left it with Him. I did not bring it up on Sunday with the others in our fellowship as I did not know where I was going and so felt that I only had half the story. All of my possessions were in boxes, yet I did not know where to go. I was trusting in God and waiting upon His next move, but as the six weeks turned into four days I admit to feeling anxious. I also prompted Terry and Karen that time was nearly up and with only two days to go they found a flat. I asked if they could help me out by taking in Flopsy the dogsy and they were quite happy about it.

An Offer Of Accommodation

That evening a guy from the fellowship rang named Leslie. It was a surprise as I hadn't given out my number or the fact that I was moving – only two people there knew. He was phoning to ask if I had anywhere to go when it was time to move out, of course I didn't so I jumped at the chance to stay at his and gave him and God my biggest 'thank you'. Well, if you recall I had promised God that I would go anywhere and this seemed to be His prompt to go somewhere particular for a reason. It transpired that Leslie's garage had been full until today, so I could work hard on moving all of my stuff out. At the start of December all three of us moved out of my bungalow Sandboy and I moved in with Leslie.

Very soon after moving in with him I soon found out that Leslie had a serious drink problem and after two days he took to his bed for a full fortnight. He ate nothing and lost two stones. He claimed to see a demon standing at the bottom of his bed. So it finally clicked with me that God had prompted him to contact me as a way of putting me in his life and now it is my turn to do something. My new routine was to go to work each morning, come home and find a way to feed him. He was in a terrible way, drinking heavily and talking to himself about his son Kyle coming to stay over Christmas. I used to berate him, saying that Kyle wouldn't want to see his Dad in this condition, and I would pray over him that God would move His grace and mercy within Leslie and that he would be healed of this drink problem. I guessed that there was a lot of work ahead, but God had indeed put me here.

After some days there was a tiny little improvement giving me hope that I could come back from work early, check on Leslie, shower, then pop up to Cheltenham to see Rachel, who was living with Amanda, her Mum. Rachel was in her school play and of course this proud Dad very much wanted to see that. When I arrived home Leslie was in a terrible state. I was still in my work clothes, trying to calm him down when my daughter rang up and asked if Daddy was coming to the school play. I explained that my friend was really ill and looks like I won't make it. She was upset and said "Dad, I have bought you the last seat, number one hundred." All of a sudden a picture filled my mind of what the school hall looked like in great detail, immediately I said "Darling, I am coming. I will be there at 7 o'clock." It was now 17:45 and the school was eighty miles away.

I turned to Leslie and said "I know you need me, but my daughter needs me." I rang my mate Dave to come round and sit with Leslie, showered, jumped in the van and hoofed it to Cheltenham. On a normal day you would put aside around two hours for the journey, I now had about one hour. Halfway there I ran into road works, heavy traffic and that should have been the time to truly start the panicking but this time I didn't as I really felt that God had matters in hand. I recalled the times that God provided when needed, not before; so I prayed whilst at the wheel "God, I know you want me there and Lord, I know that You are going make it happen. This cannot happen by my own cleverness or strength, but all things are possible in Yours."

Now this is what happened next, and may God be my witness and judge what I say, this is the truth. I do not remember the journey after that point. All I knew was arriving at the village of North Leech at 18:55 and there in the dark my step-son Paul was standing on the corner — I have no idea why he was standing there. He hopped in the van and directed me to the school and we were there in three minutes. I was in the hall bang on 19;00 and what an evening it had been. First the vision from God, second the missing half of the journey, thirdly Paul just standing on the road side and lastly, when I was in the hall, I could see that it was exactly as had been laid out by the vision earlier on. Bonus! I was right by a power socket so I could plug in the camcorder. Once again God's timing and way of doing things worked out perfectly, I was simply swept along by His plan.

What about this second half of the journey? I simply don't know what had happened, but was put in mind of this.

> *"And when they were come up out of the water, the Spirit of the Lord caught away Philip, that the eunuch saw him no more: and he went on his way rejoicing."*
> - Acts 8:39 KJV.

Arriving back at Leslie's I was full of the evening and wanting to share the wonder of God with anyone who was in my way. It seemed to have an effect on Leslie and he declared an intention to give up drink and recover his health. Well it did happen and over the next fortnight there was a marked improvement as he gave up drink, cleaned himself up and indeed his son Kyle came to stay for Christmas.

I took Rachel and we stayed at my Mum's for two weeks. Arriving back at Leslie's he was really doing well. Alcoholism is such a complicated subject and recovery has to go through many stages, but it appeared that my part in one step was now complete and in my prayer time God said that it was time for me to move on. I was a bit surprised as I had thought that I was to be with Leslie for quite some time longer than this. So I took a moment and then asked God when I should move. I waited for about 10 minutes before God said "Roy, you are to move on February 13th." The next day was Saturday so I talked it over with Leslie but did not mention the date, I wanted Leslie independently to tell me the same date. Leslie asked if I had had enough of him but I said "You know I haven't, but I did tell you it would only be short term and when God calls me then it is time to move on." He said OK and I went to work to finish off a job. I was about to go home when God spoke to me and said "Jesus came to serve and not to be served." These words stopped me dead in my tracks. They appeared to be confirmation that it was indeed time to move on. I had been put with Leslie to help and serve him, but now that he was better he was starting to look after me.

Back at his house Leslie said that Mike had rung and would like to meet up for a pint. I changed clothes and went to meet Mike. As we were talking he paused then seated himself further back in his chair and said "Do you know what, Roy, Jesus came to serve and not to be served." My jaw hit the floor and my eyes fell out of their wide open sockets and rolled under the table. I replied "Mike, God spoke those exact words to me this morning at work. God is amazing in the way that He works in our lives. For me this is secondary confirmation that it is time to move on."

Two weeks later we went out again and Mike drove me and two others home. I was seated in the rear of the car and there was a lot of talking but I kept quiet. God spoke and said "Don't share with others, but share everything with me."

Leslie was still up and said that he was fine. He was thinking about me moving on so I said "What date are you thinking?" You will remember that I was waiting for him to suggest February 13th. He said "Well, Kyle is coming to stay on February 15th for the half term week, would February 13th be good for you?" I did not tell him what God had said in the car but simply said "yes". He asked if I had anywhere to go and I said "No, but the Lord will provide". Every day for the next two weeks Leslie asked me if I had anywhere to go. With two nights to go Leslie went out to a quiz with Terry and Karen. They asked if I wanted to come but I said I fancied a quiet night in. I needed to have some time with God. It is difficult to move somewhere if you don't know where to go. Yes, there were two days left for an answer to arrive, but the old human anxiety was kicking in.

Prayer did not yield an answer so I went to the kitchen to prepare lunch for tomorrow at work, as I did this I was still praying "Lord, you promise to answer our prayers when we pray in faith." As soon as I said the last word the phone rang, it was my friend Martin back in my old village of Sandbay. Once again, how he had Leslie's number or knew that I was there was something of a mystery. Martin said he was thinking about me when he opened a cupboard and a piece of paper fell out with my name on it, so he took this as a sign to ring me. We had a good general chat but there were no clues about moving on and Martin was not a Christian, though a very nice man. Then he put Tracey his wife on the phone. Tracey was a Christian and lovely woman. She asked how long I would be staying with Leslie and I said that I would be moving out very soon. Straight away she asked if I had anywhere to go and if not I was to move in with them and that I was to think about it. I replied "Tracey I have thought about it." I told her about what Martin had said about the piece of paper, how he had rung just as I said the word "faith" and that this offer was perfectly timed. I believed with all of my heart that this was God's design and timing and that you can't go wrong following God and told this to Tracey.

Asking her when it was possible to move in she suggested February 13th. God is indeed my strength and helper in times of need. When Leslie came back I told him and he was able to offer thanks to God. God wants us to trust in Him even when we have to wait for Him, even if it means receiving your answer right at the last minute. God wants you to trust Him during those periods that our own nature would have us panicking, then you more fully appreciate the power of the Holy Spirit in your life. If I had not had an answer by February 13th I would certainly have questioned my correct hearing of God, but I knew that it was God because the Holy Spirit that is within testified that it was so. Secondly, the business of selling the bungalow had started barely six months into being a Christian. I had had confirmation about this twice on a Sunday and the answers were the same: "Let go and follow Him and I will catch you."

Dear Reader, may I ask you something today? Where are you today with God? Is He leading you? Is He speaking to you? When was the last time He spoke to you? Can you remember the first time that God touched your life? Can you recall becoming a Christian and God's Holy Spirit coming upon you? Has your life changed so that all you want to do is tell people about Christ? I know that the seed of life is within me and when I die I have the confidence that I will go into the presence of the Lord.

> *"We are confident, and willing rather to be absent from the body, and to be present with the Lord."*
> - 2 Corinthians 5:8 KJV.

Have you that assurance today? Once I was listening to a preacher and two teenage girls in the crowd asked him if it was OK to go to a disco. He said that it was fine, and he knew that some preachers would have said no and slapped the Bible but he didn't as he knew that these girls had the seed of life within them, and when they would go to the disco that they would take Jesus with them. At the next meeting they said that they had been but had come home early and of course the preacher asked why. They said "Jesus did not like it."

How you interpret the voice of God within you depends on many things, for these two girls it was a straightforward interpretation of Jesus and His likes and this worked well for them.

A Prayer

- O Lord Jesus Christ our God, Who for the sake of Your eternal mercy and loving kindness became man, and suffered crucifixion and death for the salvation of all; Who rose from the dead and ascended into heaven, and sits on the right hand of the Father, where You hear the prayers of all who call upon You humbly and with their whole heart: incline Your ear to us, and hear the prayers that Your unworthy servants offer as a spiritual sacrifice for all Your people.

Back In Sandbay

Having moved out of Leslie's and in with Tracey and Martin I found myself back in my home village of Sandbay. It was tempting to think that by going back I wasn't making progress, but I was learning to allow myself to relax into the idea that God wanted me there. After all, there was no reason to be anywhere else. I soon found that my little rent money played an important part in the household, but I wonder if my presence was causing friction between the two as they would often have words. In the end I asked us all to pray together and they said that they loved me being there. I was there for about two months. Once I went into town to meet Terry and Karen; they had decided to move to Ireland and needed to give Flopsy back. Tracey and Martin had their own dog so that would not work out. I went to pick up Flopsy in the van once again with no actual plan.

Vanessa And Flopsy

On the way back through Sandbay I saw Tracey and her son James and Tracey's friend Vanessa all out for a walk. Back at the house I went upstairs to the bathroom and locked the door as I needed some urgent prayer. I said "Lord, I know it is short notice and You know that my little dog Flopsy is in the van and that he cannot stay here. Could you please find him somewhere to live? Amen." Coming out of the bathroom I bumped into James who said "Do you want your dog? We noticed him in your van when you drove past and my Mum's friend Vanessa said that she would like him." What could I say? I met Vanessa who seemed nice and she loved Flopsy so a few minutes later she walked away with my ex-dog. A total breaking with Flopsy was not what I had envisaged and it hurt but the timing was perfect, so time to buckle down and follow the bigger plan.

Martin found work, easing money pressures and the atmosphere improved. I knew that the accommodation was short-term, but the lovely couple seemed to be becoming accustomed to my presence, so I added the matter to regular prayer. But I found it quite difficult as lots of distractions kept coming to mind and there was an internal voice saying "You are coming home, soon." I asked God if this meant that I was going to die soon, but felt quite unsettled about it all. It didn't have the calm authority of God's usual direction. My Christian friends did not know what to make of it. Continuing to feel concerned I made some special time for prayer and poured out my heart to God and then, as is my wont, waited quietly for God. In due course this reference washed over me.

> *"And he said unto them, Verily I say unto you, that there be some of them that stand here, which shall not taste of death, till they have seen the kingdom of God come with power."*
>
> - Mark 9:1 KJV.

This is a complicated verse to do with God's Kingdom. I took it that the relevance to me is that I was not to die immediately and I would live to see more of the wonders of God.

Two weeks later Rachel and I drove to Bedfordshire to see my Mum for the weekend and we slept on the floor. Early in the morning God prompted me and said "Roy, Rachel loves you so much that she is prepared to sleep on the floor so that she can spend time with you." I looked wonderingly at my daughter asleep on the floor. Then came a second communication "It is time for you to buy a house." Over breakfast I shared this with the two ladies of the house and they were both pleased.

Buying 5 Court Place

Arriving back at Tracey and Martin's they expressed happiness at my being there and their looking forward to me being with them for Christmas in four months. In my bedroom I presented this to God as He had instructed me to move on and my two good friends wanting me to stay around. Starting on Monday I went house-hunting, allowing the process to be directed by God. In the estate agents I asked about any two bedroomed semi-detached. The agent said that they had one house, 5 Court Place. I went to view, loved it, put in an offer. Usual problem, £4,000 more than I could afford and the mortgage carried from the old property wouldn't cover it. But the feeling that all was in God's hands carried me along so the next day back at the estate agent's I went back to tell them that I will take the house, trusting in God to make things happen. The agent looked at me and said "Do you want it at the old price or the new one? The price has been reduced by £4,000." It seemed like praises to God were due sooner than I could have anticipated.

Given how generous and warm Tracey and Martin had been to me I was nervous of telling them the news. However when I arrived there that night Tracey said "Have you thought about buying your own place?" I thought about how amazing is God as He had clearly prepared the way. So I told her the news and there was general happiness all round.

I don't believe that these things are coincidences, God is a God of wonder and wants to be involved in all of our lives. We can choose to have a little piece of that wonder or a larger, but why go small? Go for the bigger picture and don't miss out. Get involved with God and He can map a plan for your life in which trust and blessing go together.

Jimmy Prays

On a different occasion I went to a prayer meeting with my brother-in-law Mike and his friend Jimmy. I had heard lots of testimonies from Jimmy about God working in his life and I asked Jimmy to pray for me as I wanted in on that action. I sat in a chair whilst he prayed for me. It felt like I was being emptied from the inside and quite light headed. Thirty minutes later Jimmy had departed but I stayed seated as I felt so heavy that I could not stand or leave the seat. I felt drained and stuck down. Eventually I was able to rise and then swapped from feeling heaviness to a light floating feeling. It was most enjoyable floating in the presence of God.

Moving House – A Three Year Project

Back to the new house. Two weeks later I moved in and Rachel and Mum helped with the shifting. I had been about a year living out of a suitcase so of course I was excited to have my own home and privacy back again, but that year had been a steep learning curve and training about living by faith and it had taken me out of my comfort zone to live by obedience and see the resultant blessings.

On that day that I moved in I stepped over the threshold and had another heavenly prompt "You will only live in this house for three years". As I told my Mum everything that had happened to me I also told her this. Though not a Christian she took a great interest in my new life in Jesus and of course I always prayed for her.

This new house was just around the corner from where I worshipped, otherwise I had no idea what was my purpose in this new location. Sometimes God makes things clear, sometimes not; you have to wait for direction and clarification and live by faith. I am put in mind of Moses and how he felt when God directed him to go to Pharaoh and say "Let my people go!" Moses had a speech impediment and was not a likely public speaker, but God blessed Moses and made it all work out.

> *"But Moses said to the people, "Take courage! Stand, and see the deliverance from God that he will perform for you today. For as you have seen the Egyptians today, you shall not ever again see them time without end. The Lord will fight for you, and you will be quiet."*
> *- Exodus 14:13 LXX.*

Moses had a firm and unshakeable faith and he was faithful to God. But when the Egyptians were chasing and were close behind and they came to the Red Sea Moses still cried out to God. To the human eye there seemed to be no escape and they envisaged being caught between slaughter and drowning.

> *"Then the Lord said to Moses, "Why are you crying out to me? Speak to the sons of Israel, and let them break camp. And you, raise your rod, and stretch out your hand over the sea, and break it apart, and let the sons of Israel enter into the midst of the sea on what was dry."*
> *- Exodus 14:15 LXX.*

God wants obedience, but not out of any sense of ego, only so that we can see how a life driven by His Holy Spirit and being in that place where God directs leads to blessings and awe of God's wisdom and power. Even the skills that we have are useless if we are not in the right place at the right time. And where is that? Only God knows.

Les

Three months after moving in it was Good Friday 1998. It seemed like nothing was happening, but I wanted to be useful to God. As I looked out of the bedroom window at the new cul-de-sac in which I found myself living I made a prayer to God that I am available for Him, today if He wants. Being a Good Friday I popped around the corner to my worship group to help out. A cup of tea and a hot cross bun on offer to all visitors. I was given a position by the tea hatch.

In came a man walking very slow, dishevelled, unshaven and looking down on his luck. I asked God if I could help out and speak to him. The man came over for a cup of tea and said that he might then be going. I felt the heavenly nudge to stick with him so I said "I'll come with you." He said he that was going to the shop and even though it was only one hundred and fifty yards away it took us twenty minutes at his speed. At the shop he didn't buy food, as I expected but two bottles of whisky. I didn't comment and then we went to his house, a short journey but about an hour on foot, and guess what, he lived across from me. I realised that here is the reason in front of me why God has placed me in 5 Court Place.

In his house it truly stank and I felt that I wouldn't be able to breathe. I had to hold a cloth over my mouth whilst trying not to embarrass him. We went into the long kitchen with every work surface covered in empty whisky bottles. It was evident that this man had a serious problem. When I left I said "I will see you later" and rather surprisingly he gave me a front door key.

This man's name is Les and his story is wonderful and I love sharing it. To this day we joke about the day he came in for a free cup of tea and a hot cross bun and the fact that in due time he received a whole lot more than that. I do hope that his story thrills you as much as it thrilled me.

Later that day I did indeed come back to see Les and he was smashed out of his brains, so we developed a pattern where I would sit with him and try to sober him up. This went on for weeks. He claimed that he wanted to give up drink but didn't know how to. We have already noted that alcoholism is a complicated disease and requires a lengthy process of management and recovery. He had been on the bottle for ten years every single night.

My Walk With Jesus

We became very good friends as I visited him every evening. He begged me to give him a drink and I always said "No, you can have tea, coffee or milk but no whisky." Then the next day I would go and see him after work and he had somehow procured another bottle from the shop. I later found out that it was being delivered on account of his bad walking. One Sunday I went round but was accosted by Les' neighbour, she said "What influence are you putting on Les? He has been banging and crashing around and fighting with his brother. He beat him up and put him in a home. Les is an alcoholic and no one can help him. I've tried but he is a mess." I let her run out of words whilst standing still and looking at her. I said "God has put me here to help, because God cares about Les and wants to improve his life and be part of it." I mentioned some of the things that God had done for me, then went in to see Les. He always slept on the sofa as he found it hard to climb the stairs and he was asleep there now and totally out of it. I decided to go around the corner to our worship group and returned a couple of hours later.

By this time Les was still on the sofa but awake with one eye open, the other stuck closed and it was clear that he was in a lot of pain. He asked me to help him. The heavenly inspiration stuck again and I went to bring Julian, our pastor. We stayed with Les for three and a half hours until Les had almost sobered up. We talked about the Gospel and the healing power of Christ. I said to Les "You asked for help, I utterly believe that Christ helps those who have faith in Him. Is there any reason why you shouldn't give your life to Christ?" He put his hands in the air as it to say "no reason" and said "none at all." I led him in prayer to God, mentioning that Christ died for our sins. Les repeated after me and gave his life to God. This is a special moment and certainly does not mean that all of our problems are immediately solved, but now that we are able to work with God and ask Him for help in sorting out issues.

Another heavenly prompt to put my hand on Les' back and pray for him. It was obvious that he had medical problems, though I didn't know what they were – apart from the drink. So I asked God to set about delivering Les from drink and his back problems. Julian was happy to let me take the lead in the prayer. Eventually it was late and we had to go home. Les was seated with a blanket over his legs, so Julian and I said that we would let ourselves out, but Les said "No, I will see you out." As he stood up his back made one massive cracking sound and instead of standing in his usual rounded position he stood straight. We all looked at each other and said "Did you hear that?" Les walked in a normal way to show us out and said that he no longer had any back pain.

We later learned that Les had had five vertebrae gone in the lower part of his spine, he was on pain killers that I saw were the size of gob-stoppers and was being given morphine for the pain. Additionally he wore a girdle for support, but as we have already seen he was able to walk, but it was so slow that he was barely able to take two steps without pausing. I did not know all this till later but it quickly became apparent that that night God had decided that it was time and so healed Les of his back problem and also the ten year drink addiction. All this in one go at the very start of Les' Christian life.

The next day I called to see Julian so we could pray for Les. I was mindful of the ongoing nature of alcoholism and that Les might be tempted to undo God's work so I asked God that if Les ever succumbed to drink that the whisky would taste bitter and sour in his mouth. Following this I went to see Les. He opened the door himself and the first thing he said was "I have a confession to make, I had a drop of whisky but it tasted bitter and sour in my mouth, so I poured it away." I told Les what had happened before I arrived and my belief that as Les had used the exact same phrase "bitter and sour" that this was evidence of God at work healing Les. As always it was amazing to me to be able to witness another of God's miracles.

Over the next couple of days Les started to remember more and to have more feeling in his body. His right hand had been broken and was in a mess, not properly healed. He said this was a result of his beating his brother Percy when they fought over a bottle of whisky five years ago. Social Services had split them up told them not to meet each other again and Percy was put into a home. Les' hand had not healed and he was on more pain killers for that. He had visited hospital but they said that five years was too long to leave it and there was no longer anything that could be done so keep on taking the pain killers.

These consultants who earn a tremendous amount of money were certain that there was nothing that could be done. As I have previously said I believe where you put your last word is where you put your faith. So what if the doctors have said that there is nothing more that can be done, what then? Perhaps you might ask for a second opinion, but what if that agrees with the first? All these things had been going around in Les' mind comparing it to the previous evening when, he believed, it was in return for giving his life to Jesus that he had received healing for his back and his addiction. He asked me pray for his hand. I was not even in the house, actually still on the doorstep when Les asked this, it was clearly of immediate concern to him. It was something of a moment and I was mindful of the Gospel reports of Jesus restoring withered and deformed hands providing the example, so I prayed for Les' hand to be restored in Jesus' name.

The next day after work I went around again and may God be my witness and judge and the only Lover and Healer of mankind, Les' hand was totally restored. Praise God. God created all flesh and it is obedient to Him and if you let Him He will apply healing to your life.

The Car Announces Its Imminent Death

A week later Rachel and I went back up to my Mum's and we had a great time. Just as I was preparing to leave my car made serious and expensive sounding noises. I told my Mum that I would ring her when I arrived home and Rachel said "If we get home." I replied that I believed that we would be fine as all these things are in Jesus' hands and He is far more powerful than cars. At first the car seemed fine and little Rachel went to sleep. At one point we were following a lorry so I changed down into third gear preparing to overtake. Just as I started the manoeuvre the engine made a bang loud enough to wake Rachel and then a grinding noise. Rachel asked what it was and I said "Nothing to worry about, it's only the engine." Then I took a moment to contemplate what an idiot I am and what stupid things I am saying, clearly the engine is a big item to worry about.

Then I heard God's voice, after all the times that He graced me with the gift of hearing Him I took immediate comfort. He said "If you keep it to under 60 mph and no more, then I will take care of the rest." I offered a heart felt "Thank You. I shall do exactly that." I kept a close eye on the speed and did not once exceed 60 mph all the way home. I dropped Rachel off with her mother in

North Leach with the car still going and set off back home to Weston-Super-Mare, about another two hours run. Halfway at Stroud the heater started blowing cold. I knew that there was a severe problem but had no alternative other than to trust in God and instead of making a run for it, instead obey the Almighty and keep it under 60 mph. I don't think that the speed was the important matter, it could have been any speed. What God wanted was obedience and reliance upon Him.

As I went along the temperature gauge started to rise until it was about on the red so I said a little prayer to God to remind Him of the deal that He had promised: He would see me home as long as I didn't exceed the speed that He had given me, and by the way the temperature gauge is going up and I am worried about it. As soon as I finished my little speech the needle went down to very cold and it stayed there for forty-five minutes until I arrived home. As I turned into the cul-de-sac the temperature started to rise and in the few yards to my house it was boiling hot. When parked I lifted the bonnet to check the water level and it was totally dry; so I poured in more water only to see it immediately pour out of the water pump and that the pump belt had broken. The important thing to me was that God took me home safe and I wasn't stranded in the middle of nowhere.

It certainly makes the blood pump to live on the edge like this, fighting my own human instinct to panic and instead to remember to ask God all the time for assistance. He really does care for us and all the little things in our lives.

One new water pump and belt later and the car was fine, no damage at all. An extra blessing, thank you God. I am pretty sure that driving for forty-five minutes or more with no water should have destroyed the engine. But God was in control of bringing me home because I gave Him the situation.

Dear Reader, are you letting God take control of your situations and are you letting Him bring you home?

"O taste and see that the Lord is good."
- Psalms 33:9 LXX.

Over time it became more natural for me to turn to God many times per day. I trusted that it was appropriate to spread the news of God everywhere, including at work and so I talked to as many people as possible outlining the benefits of a life in God, how God wants to help them and how lost we all are without Christ as the focus of our being.

A Prayer
• Remember first of all Your Holy, Universal and Apostolic Church, that You have purchased with Your precious blood. Strengthen it, multiply it, keep it in peace, and do not allow the gates of hell to stand against it. Heal the schisms of the churches, stop the raging of the heathen, root out and cleanse all heresies, destroying them by the power of Your Holy Spirit.

Terry The Fork Lift Driver
Around July 1998 I was on a site fitting kitchens when the fork lift driver, Terry, called me over. He looked terribly unhappy and asked if I was a Christian. He said that he wasn't but asked me if I believed that God could do anything. Of course I said yes. "Right," he said "pray for me. I am fed up with my job and want a change and if your God is as good as you say He is, He will find me one, won't He?" I asked Terry if he had been looking for a job already and he said no and then more insistence that God would do it for him. Furthermore "If God answers this prayer you can baptise me over there in that water butt and I will become a church-goer."

So we prayed and two days later a friend of his phoned up who offered him a job. Terry was excited when he told me of this and I asked him what he was going to do. He said that he had accepted it and was now working out his notice. "So," I said "where do you want to be baptised?" He said "No, no, it's alright, thanks anyway." Terry wanted the blessings of God, but he didn't want God, even though God is watching each one of us, waiting for when we are ready to offer that free interaction with Him and discover that in return for our pitiful contributions to the deal, that He is a good God and Lover of mankind.

Looking back to the time that I was a non-believer and enemy of the Gospel it is clear that sometimes God still listened to me and answered those prayers. Eventually I learned the point and gave my life to God and what a great and exciting journey it has been and continues to be. I trust in Him to death, and beyond.

A Plumber With No Work

A week later I found myself on a different site several miles away in Portishead and I was soon recognised on site and soon I was awarded the nickname of "The Preacher". I suppose that I liked the soubriquet as I started thinking of myself as a part-time carpenter and a full-time preacher. I certainly loved doing the latter more than the former.

In one of the houses that we were building on-site I was with three plumbers. I was downstairs putting in some stud walls and they were upstairs sitting on the joists putting in the pipework, so I could not help but overhear their conversations about the lack of money and their prices being too low and that this would force them to move on. Two plumbers then went home. The one that was left had a little work to do to finish off and he repeated matters to me. I offered that God could help anyone and asked if he was a Christian. He wasn't but as I was I told him the Gospel and that God could help in any situation. He asked how we could tell God about this need and I led him in prayer and he added that, being short of money, that he would quite appreciate a job by Friday. I thought to myself that this was turning into quite the shopping list, I am used to praying for my own needs and then waiting for the answer, sometimes for a while. He had a job offer, not on the Friday that he wanted, but the day after. A friend in the pub asked him to come and work for him on Monday. He even received a company car. I don't know what happened after that, whether he thanked God or became a Christian, but I am sure that God was watching him and was ready for when the one-sided relationship became two-sided.

Tony The Painter

Two days later I was sent to another site and at break time had a seat with the painters. Tony was a big guy both in height and girth. For him bending down to paint the skirting boards was a real problem and he looked to be in pain. I asked him if he shouldn't be resting at home, but he said that he had a heavy mortgage so had to carry on working to pay it. He would work until the pain overcame him, then sit down for five minutes before continuing with much groaning when he bent over and the pain on his face told the story.

After watching enough of this I asked Tony if he would mind

me praying for his back problem; he smiled and his expression said "What have we got here?" But he said "yes, why not?" but kept on working. He simply had no interest in the prayer that I said for him. At the end he said "If that doesn't work, nothing will." I replied that there was nothing that I could do, but I know a God who can.

The next day he came to work and I saw him step out of his car, and moving freely, carry his tools into the house and start work on the skirting boards without any problems. I asked him about his back and he said that it was fine as he had been rubbing cream onto it. I said that it was not the cream and that there is no point in worshipping the cream when it is God that has healed you. He considered me but did not say anything, so I could only pray that he would realise that the source of his blessings had come from heaven, not from a little plastic pot.

After a few days another painter started on site and at break time we would sit together whilst I told him about God whilst, like many others, he laughed at me. But this didn't put me down as I remembered that I was trying to be like Jesus, that He took a lot worse abuse than I and He did not take offence. After all that I have seen about putting trust in God and then seeing His power in action some laughter from a non-believer is hardly going to sway me.

Then Tony came in and said "Something strange happened to me last night. Listen to this. I went home a couple of Fridays ago and the wife and I had a big row and then we didn't speak for a full two weeks. Last night I came home and it was still icy silent so I thought 'blow this' and went off to the pub. As I was driving there came a little voice into my head 'Ask God for help' so I said a prayer in the car 'Please God, can you do something about the quietness at home." Ten minutes later I was in the pub with a pint when my mobile phone rang, it was my wife, she said 'Are you coming home Darling? Your dinner is ready.' What do you make of all that?"

Tony was completely blown over by what had happened. I said to him "You asked God to do something about the quietness in your house and He did." Again Tony just looked at me then carried on working. One thing is for certain, he could not deny what had happened. No matter how it happened, the fact that he prayed and ten minutes later it was answered remains.

"For many are called, but few are chosen."
- Matthew 22:14 KJV.

Dear Reader, if these stories have already convinced you of the reality of God then this day could be your turning point to follow Christ. If not, well then, I have plenty more stories to relate.

A Prayer

- Have mercy, O Lord, upon our Royal family, our ministers, and all in civil authority, and save them, together with the armed forces of our country. Give them peace and continual victory over injustice and evil in all places. May they keep Your holy Church secure, that all Your people may live calm and ordered lives in Your sight, in true faith and prayer, with godly deeds.

Dave Furnishes A Rabbit Hutch

That weekend Rachel came to visit. She was in the market for a pet rabbit so we found one that she liked from the pet store and together we started work on a hutch.

On Monday I was moved to another site. It is the normal lot of the jobbing carpenter to move around and I see it as a series of opportunities to spread the Gospel. I knew some of the other tradesmen on site. Whilst working I was thinking about the rabbit hutch, it was nearly done but required mesh for the door and window. I was wondering where I could find just enough for these tiny gaps as a whole roll was a lot of money and way more than needed. Naturally I raised the matter in prayer and then the heavenly voice "There will be some at work." I replied back that it seemed unlikely as we don't use mesh at work. This was naughty of me, to question God, I should be instinctively trusting Him in all things by now. So I caught myself, said sorry, and asked where should I find it at work. God said "Go and see Dave." There was only one Dave, a painter, and that didn't seem a right source for mesh, so I asked the question again, and again the same reply. I was shocked at my own lack of trust so opted to go and see Dave right away and try to make up for my bad behaviour.

Finding Dave, I asked if he had any mesh at home. He said that he had a roll at home and how much did I need? God is my amazing provider. Dave brought in the roll the next day and gave me enough for the rabbit hutch. Then I told Dave how I knew to ask him and talked about God for a while. Dave said that he had a back problem and would I pray for him. The next day I had to go back to the other building site so I did not find out what happened with his back, but I was given to understand that when I prayed for him that Dave felt it and a shudder went through him. I believe that he was healed and that was why I was put on that site for such a short time, not just for a bit of mesh.

Dear Reader, God knows everything about you. He knows what you are going to do before you think of it. Before Rachel ever mentioned a rabbit God knew that I would be asking about mesh. God knew that he would introduce me to Dave and that I would want to pray for him. My God is the only God and Jesus Christ is the Son of the Living God. Could I ask you, where do you stand in relation to God's Kingdom? Does the Holy Spirit lead you?

> *"For as many as are led by the Spirit of God, they are the sons of God."*
> - Romans 8:14 KJV.

Would you say that you are in or out of the Kingdom? Only you know.

> *"Acknowledge the Lord, and call on his name. Sing to Him, and make music to Him; tell of all His wonderful things. Be commended in His holy name; let the heart of people that seek the Lord be glad. Seek the Lord and be strengthened; seek His face continually."*
> - Psalm 104:1-4 LXX.

I hope that you have the patience to continue reading about my life and my walk with Jesus. I am not an eloquent or educated man, all I have is my enthusiasm for my Lord and God and a genuine desire to tell of the many blessings given to me. As of writing I have been a Christian for about twenty-five years, so I am young in the faith and lack spiritual maturity. Age does not always bring maturity, although with enough time I hope to learn a thing or two. What also matters is how much and how fast you want to grow. For me, when Christ entered my life He was more real than life itself.

One of the stories in the Bible that really inspires me is in the book of Numbers 13-27. It is too big to quote here, please allow my condensed version. There were twelve spies who worked for Moses, one from each tribe of Israel. They were sent to spy out the land of Canaan, that is, the land promised to Israel, but already inhabited. Upon their return they all gave their reports. Ten spies said that the land could not be taken as a race of giants called the Nephilim were there. And they started grumbling and arguing, but Caleb and Joshua wanted to take the land for God. Caleb silenced the people and Moses stood up to talk "We should go up and take possession of the land, for we can certainly do it." But because of the fear and unbelief of the people God allowed them to remain camped in the desert for forty years and that entire generation died natural deaths in the desert with only Caleb and Joshua entering the promised land, along with the new generation. Even Moses did not enter the land, on account of a previous transgression and disbelief.

> "But as for my servant Caleb, because there was another spirit in him and he followed me, I too will bring him into the land, there where he entered, and his offspring shall inherit it."
> - Numbers 14:24 LXX.

Caleb displayed maturity. He was not blinded by fear or unbelief or discouragement. He wanted to take the land when God told them to, so showing obedience. Sometimes we face huge problems in our lives that look as insurmountable as giants. How do we deal with them? Do we worry, do nothing or think "why me?" Perhaps we might even blame God. We are told what we ought to do, put on the armour of God and let Him fight your battles.

> "Put on the whole armour of God, that you may be able to stand against the wiles of

the devil. For we wrestle not against flesh and blood, but against principalities, against powers, against the rulers of the darkness of this world, against spiritual wickedness in high places. Wherefore take unto you the whole armour of God, that you may be able to withstand in the evil day, and having done all, to stand.
                                    - Ephesians 6:11-13 KJV.

Up to this point in my stories I had been a Christian for five years and am learning to trust in God, sometimes immediately, sometimes after battling with the human instinct to doubt. However God has always brought me through.

Render judgement, O Lord, on those who do me wrong; fight against those who fight against me! Take hold of buckler and shield and rise up to help me! Extend a sword, and block against my pursuers; say to my soul, "I am your deliverance."
                                    - Psalms 34:1-4 LXX.

Each one of us goes through hard times, the question is how do you deal with them. Again I repeat "Where you put your last word is where you put your faith." My life's lessons in suffering, trying to go my own way instead of God's way, has shown me that one goes no-where. Additionally it appears to me that God uses one's suffering to draw one to Him. Suffering, often through our own wilfulness in entering the state, or trying to use one's own skills to escape from it, helps us to be more open to God's still quiet voice calling to us. Most people call upon the Name of the Lord when they are at their lowest. It is indeed when you are at your lowest that your barriers are lowered and God's strength is clearest and, once allowed into your life, that He can begin the work of healing and rebuilding. As I look back on my life I can see the years that I have wasted going my way, because I did not have my eyes on God but only on the world. Since I moved my focus to God and started reading the Bible, and listening to what God is saying to me, and practising being faithful to Him; since all of those things started to happen then I have witnessed God's grace at work in myself and in others.

> *"I am come that they might have life, and that they might have it more abundantly."*
> *- John 10:10 KJV.*

It is a great journey because I am not alone. Jesus satisfies my needs, Jesus keeps me safe and I look forward to salvation, that includes being in heaven after an earthly death. God cares about healing in this life and salvation in the next.

> *"That if you shall confess with your mouth the Lord Jesus, and shall believe in your heart that God has raised him from the dead, you shall be saved."*
> *- Romans 10:9 KJV.*

Dear Reader, God is keen that we enter into a relationship with Him and become able to converse. I, myself, love talking with God because He listens to me and I am always learning how to pause in silence and await the replies. The health of my prayer life is important to me and those times when God keeps silence concern me. If you are in a position to say that you speak with God and you have acted upon this in faith then you will be able to remember the blessings that followed.

> *But without faith it is impossible to please Him: for he that cometh to God must believe that He is, and that He is a rewarder of them that diligently seek Him.*
> *- Hebrews 11:6 KJV.*

If you do not know God then it would be the best present that you could give to yourself to seek Him. Each one of us has a spiritual void in our lives and, like living with an injury, we become used to living with it. We often overdevelop an interest to compensate for that feeling of emptiness with things such as sport, TV, computers, video games. Whatever we use it doesn't last. What is new and exciting today is old and tired tomorrow.

Whatever the world offers you for diversion and immersion will only work for a short time until the new model comes out. It is like chasing the wind and even the most stubborn of us cannot avoid learning that we are going nowhere. To put it another way; if you spread yourself over all of these distractions then you will be weak in distribution. To gather yourself back into one unity and place yourself in God is a path of healing. A relationship with God lasts forever; He will never let you down; He will always support your efforts to fulfil the potential with which you were created. This relationship will last forever, past your own death and when you are reunited with your body.

As I continue to share with you episodes from my life and my own spiritual development I hope that it will encourage and inspire you in Godly matters. My experience tells me that following Christ is a good thing and that our ongoing improvement is a work constantly under construction. God's love, most importantly, cannot be exhausted. We will never plumb the depth of it, nor reach the top of its height. I am not writing this book for my benefit; the work that I put into this will not benefit me. If you find, or improve your relationship with God it will all be to your benefit not mine. I will not gain from your decision, only you.

A Prayer

- Have mercy, O Lord, upon the Christian patriarchs and archbishops, the metropolitans and bishops, the priests and deacons, and the whole order of Your Churches clergy. Save them whom You have established to feed Your flock, and by their prayers have mercy on us sinners, and save us.

Life In A Bypass

It was a dark and cold February evening in 1999 and I went to see my daughter. The journey was very familiar to me, having done it for eight years every other weekend. I would drive eighty miles from Weston-Super-Mare to the Cotswolds. From there another ninety miles to my Mum's in Bedfordshire where we could also see Rachel's cousins. This weekend was good, as always and on Sunday afternoon we started the journey in reverse to take Rachel back to her mother. It was already dark when we reached the Thame bypass, my daughter was asleep when the car started to slow and quickly stopped. I woke her up to tell her that the car had broken down and the first thing she said was "Say a prayer, Dad, go on, say a prayer that normally works." My goodness did that put me under pressure. I should have prayed already but when I pray it is in the expectation that God will sort everything out, which is not the same as demanding miracles. I lifted the bonnet and said a prayer whilst peering into the engine. Nothing happened.

I had no torch, no mobile phone, no breakdown cover, no cars passing which might be flagged down for assistance. My daughter was eleven and it was so dark we couldn't see each other. What should I do? I knew the road well but didn't know it's name or the nearest town. I told Rachel to sit tight and locked the car whilst I ran to the end of the road, about quarter of a mile, to see if there was any chance of help. I cannot say that this was the best thing to do, but I could not think of anything better. As I ran I could not even see myself, though the star light allowed me to see the roadside to keep on track.

After two hundred yards I thought of Rachel alone in the car and stopped. I was panicking and not relying or waiting on God. I looked up into those stars and took a moment. Eventually I found the presence of God and said: "God, help me." At that exact moment a voice near me said "Mate, do you need help?" I must have jumped as high as the stars. I was looking around in the utter blackness, unable to see my hands, when I eventually saw a solitary street light about two hundred and fifty yards away. Under the street light was the tiny figure of what might be a man. The light seemed to be shining only on him and how his voice had seemed to be right next to me was a mystery. I ran towards him and when I arrived I was hot and out of breath and gasped out "God bless you mate, you must be an angel." He didn't answer, but simply watched me as I had my hands on my knees panting away. I told him about Rachel in the broken down car and my desperation and looking for God and at that exact moment hearing his voice right next to me, and how the light was on him and nothing else and that he must be an angel sent from God. He did not comment on this but simply asked what assistance I required. I said that I need to make sure that Rachel is safe, that she arrives home safe, that I need a phone box to ring her mother, then to ring brother-in-law Mike to see if he can help. The stranger pointed to a phone box that I had not seen just a few yards away. I apologised that I did not have any money as I had spent it all on Rachel. Again he just looked at me, then said "You will not need money" and he gave me three phone cards to make my three calls.

I don't know about you, but do you know anyone who carries about one phone card, let alone three? As he passed me the three phone cards a phrase jumped into my mind 'The Father, the Son and the Holy Spirit.' I rang Amanda and told her the situation, then Mike who said that he would come if I could tell him the name of the road. Of course I didn't know so I asked the mysterious stranger who had not told me his name and he told me that this was the Thame bypass. Knowing this Mike said that he would be with us in forty-five minutes. The stranger suddenly had a 4x4 vehicle and he gave me a lift back to my car. On the short drive he said "Your daughter is fine and she knows that you are OK and will return soon."

Entering my car the first thing that Rachel said was "Dad, you left eight minutes ago but there was a voice in my head that said that you are going to be OK and will be back very soon with help." When Rachel said that I was further impressed with the goodness of God and the provision that He makes for us. Furthermore I cannot prove this to anyone, but it is my firm conviction that the stranger was an angel.

> *"Are they not all ministering spirits, sent forth to minister for them who shall be heirs of salvation?"*
> - Hebrews 1:4 KJV.

> *"Be not forgetful to entertain strangers: for thereby some have entertained angels unawares."*
> - Hebrews 13:2 KJV.

Rachel and I went to sit in the stranger's 4x4 to keep warm, and he drove us to buy fish and chips. When Mike arrived he put on a tow rope to pull us back to my Mum's. Just before we started off the stranger called me over. I thanked him profusely for all that he had done for us. He looked me straight in the eyes and said "God bless you." Then he said something that I will never forget, this time when he looked me in the eyes I felt it touch my soul, "Promise me this, if anyone ever needs help, help them." Those words went deep into me as if I were being penetrated by a very sharp sword. Why would he say this to me? It was still unproven if he was a man or actually an angel, though I believe him to be an angel, without a doubt. He stood on the roadside in the car lights and watched us being towed away until the blackness swallowed him up.

Although my engine wasn't running I had to put on my lights to be towed, and of course it meant that the brakes would not work. Praise God we didn't have to stop at any roundabout or traffic light. Just as we arrived back at my Mum's my headlights winked out. As we parked my Mum's next door neighbour was walking past and said "I thought you had gone home." I told her that we had broken down and that Mike had come to rescue us. She said "Do you have anyone to fix your car as you are far from home? If not I know someone." She rang her mechanic who took the next day off work to come and repair it. The broken part was the rotor arm and the new one cost £3.38. He did not charge me for his time. Finally we said goodbye to everyone and set off once again.

What a testimony to God's greatness. He is the greatest boss in the universe. When I was looking up to the stars the confidence came back and I knew that He would help us. I absolutely knew that he would not let us down. This is blind faith. I was able to trust that he would deliver, and He did.

> "Listen, O Lord, to my voice with which I cried aloud; have mercy on me, and listen to me! To you my heart said, "My face sought!" Your face, Lord, will I seek."
> - Psalms 26:7.

A Lost Lady Finds An Angel

The Bible is pretty insistent over the existence of angels. Would you be happy if they made themselves a part of your life and helped out from time to time?

Once I went with a friend to where he worshipped, there I talked with a lady named Sharon. I told the story above and discussed whether the mysterious stranger could have been an angel. Sharon said that she believed that he was and went on to recount her own encounter with an angel.

She said "Last year my husband and I went on holiday and we had an argument so I walked out. I walked and walked and in my anger was not taking any notice of where I was going. After two hours of walking I was calming down and then suddenly realised that I was lost. I was already emotional so I quickly started crying in the panic and fear of being lost. I asked God to help me and please to send me an angel. Then I resumed crying. Suddenly a car pulled up next to me with a lady at the wheel. She rolled down the window and said "Are you OK?" I said that I was but she still said "Can I help you? What about a lift somewhere?" Missing the opportunity right in front of my face I declined the offer. Then this lady said "Well, you did just ask for an angel." I looked at her in shock and realised that I had indeed asked for an angel, and here she was. I seated myself in her car and she set off, not asking where I would like to go.

The lady at the wheel then went on to tell me about myself, my husband and my family. I had no idea where we were going except that we were going up a hill. The lady or angel then said "When we reach the top of the hill you will see your husband walking towards us." I did not think it possible as I did not recognise the area as being near the hotel. But sure enough, at the top of the hill there was my husband. She let me out of the car and I walked back with my husband, and we talked all the way. Praise the Lord.

A Prayer
- Have mercy, O Lord, on our parents, and save them, together with our brothers and sisters, our children, our relatives and our friends. Grant them Your blessing both here and in the life to come.

Paul With A Broken Arm
That following Monday I started work on a new site outside Portishead. I loved starting new sites as it offered chances to meet new people and to tell them about the faith. I would always have my Bible with me in case of questions, and yes, there were questions as at lunchtime in the canteen the boys would gather

round to offer prayer requests as they were keen to see the results.

Sharing the faith is a two way process as it also allows me to learn something of them as individuals. One is not going to survive unless one practices what one preaches, so you have to earn the right to speak. In such crowds of forthright, hard-working, hard-drinking men it would not reflect well upon the faith were I to take offence all the time.

Once Paul, in charge of all the ground workers, had an accident and broke his arm in an awkward way requiring plaster and time off work. After about two weeks he started popping into work, just to make sure things were running smoothly. Each day at breaktime all the ground workers and myself were continuing to meet in the canteen to chat over our lunch and cup of tea. I liked the combination of food and discussion as:

> "And Jesus answered him, saying, 'It is written, that man shall not live by bread alone, but by every word of God.'"
>
> - Luke 4:4 KJV.

Paul asked me how many times I had read the Bible and whether I ever got fed up reading it. I replied that the Bible is full of life when applied to your life, it is God-breathed and brings a focus into any situation. For example, Jesus said:

> "Verily, verily, I say unto you, he that believeth on me, the works that I do shall he do also; and greater works than these shall he do; because I go unto my Father. And whatsoever you shall ask in my name, that will I do, that the Father may be glorified in the Son. If you shall ask any thing in my name, I will do it."
>
> - John 14:12-14.

Paul said that he would appreciate prayers for his arm and I said that I would. However I also believe in doing things in God's timing and not charging in when I think that the time is right. A couple of days went by and Paul asked if I had prayed for him, and then every couple of days he would ask after the prayer and complain about the pain in his arm and reported that he had to go back to hospital for more work on it and that he was frightened as there was no improvement.

It would have been easy to drag Paul off to the side, say a prayer and have it over and done with and hope that God would heal him with no feedback after that it had happened. But I have been taught to wait on the Lord, He will tell me the right time and direct me to pray when He directs that a healing will occur.

The next morning I was walking across the site when it happened. God said "Go and pray for Paul now." I looked around and Paul was a short distance away talking to five of his workers. I ran to him and, in front of everyone, said "Paul, God has just told me that now is the time. Give me your arm, I am going to pray for it." Paul was making quieting noises and saying "Not now, not now, not in front of my mates." I repeated "Paul, give me your arm now. Now is the time for God to act." And I took hold of his arm and prayed for him, for his arm, for all of his friends (who were all laughing). But I will not be offended for Christ's sake, because God is immortal and we will all fade away. When the prayer was finished I looked straight at Paul and said "God bless you, Paul."

Paul quietly stood for a moment and said "That feels better already." I said "Praise to God, praise to Jesus." He turned to all of his smirking friends and said "I am not joking, I am telling the truth, my arm is better already. There is a rushing sensation and it feels better." That night he went out and played darts using that arm and feeling very good. Praises due to God.

Word soon went around that Paul, a non-believer, was saying that after I had prayed for him that his arm was feeling a lot better. People started coming to me with prayer requests and asking for prayers for themselves. Whatever site I was working on I would ask permission to finish at midday on Friday so I could set about the long journey to pick up Rachel and go to my Mum's, but you could always bet that someone or something would get in the way. But as far as the Gospel was concerned, that is not my time – I serve the Lord. I want to see people healed and come to faith in Christ. If we can allow God to trust us with the little things, then He will eventually trust us with the larger. The currency of the spirit is faith in Christ.

John And Mini On A Tower Scaffolding

It was Friday and I was looking forward to getting away early to be with my daughter. She had taken to ringing me on my mobile to see if I had yet set off and what time she could expect me. It would take me around three hours to reach her, then another three hours to Rachel's Grandma, my Mum. I was all done and walking to the car when John the bricklayer shouted at me. He was working up a scaffold and wanted advice on how to do a roof. But as soon as he had me he changed the subject and said "I am closer to God up here." I said that it doesn't exactly work like that, but he just smiled at me. I told him and his friend Mini the labourer the way to become close to God, and that is through Jesus Christ because of His being on the Cross and trampling down death by death and dying for the sins of the world and so all of creation may regain it's rightful perfection, as God originally intended it to be, including us becoming sons and daughters of God, if we work with Him on it.

John and Mini listened but kept on working. I went on "This whole life is about Christ, and you owe it to yourself to find Him. We cannot be saved unless we first go through the process of repentance and forgiveness. We have all failed to be good people as we always serve ourselves first and that is selfishness and sin." John replied that he was not as bad as some other people, as if such a comparison could prove anything or justify his life. It only fools the person who does it into feeling better for a while. I continued "You cannot get to heaven by good works alone.

> *"As it is written, There is none righteous,*
> *no, not one."*
>
> - Romans 3:10 KJV.

"No matter how good we might think that we are, even considering how much we might help others, we are still sinners, selfish and without God. We all need repentance, forgiveness and the promise of salvation.

> *"And we have all become like unclean*
> *people; all our righteousness is like the rag*
> *of a menstruating woman."*
>
> - Isaiah 64:6 LXX.

"For all have sinned, and come short of the glory of God."
                                             - Romans 3:23 KJV.

"Sin is something that entered the world and the world is steeped in it and it affects us all and we all sin without realising what is sin.

> *"Wherefore, as by one man sin entered into the world, and death by sin; and so death passed upon all men, for that all have sinned."*
>   - Romans 5:12 KJV.

"So John, you might be thinking that if we are all sinners, how is there any chance of anyone going to heaven? There is a way.

> *"But God commendeth his love toward us, in that, while we were yet sinners, Christ died for us."*
>   - Romans 5:8 KJV.

"So you see, when Jesus defeated sin when He was on earth, He didn't sin, not even once – it would have contradicted His nature as God. He also didn't brandish His power about and though the devil recognised Christ as something special he didn't seem to recognise Christ as God, because he tried every temptation going, and then some. Christ continued to the Cross to lay down His life for all of humanity; His death vanquished sin and death and hell. This includes all of the sins that you have committed, especially those that you have kept secret that you keep hidden in darkness.

Before Christ, when people died they all went to hell. Because of His act of salvation on the Cross we now have the chance to go to heaven and enjoy the life-creating company of God."

By this time John had stopped working and was listening, though Mini the labourer kept on working.

I continued "Lads, if you died today what would be your fate?"

"For the wages of sin is death; but the gift of God is eternal life through Jesus Christ our Lord."
> \- Romans 6:23 KJV.

"So why not choose this day life instead of death? We have to come to God through Jesus on God's terms, there is no other way. Simply believe that Jesus died for our sins when He was crucified, died, was buried and rose again to life. Believe and live this life and you will ultimately be saved."

"If we confess our sins, he is faithful and just to forgive us our sins, and to cleanse us from all unrighteousness."
> \- 1 John 1:9 KJV.

"God came to earth in the person of Jesus Christ and died once and for all for us. Through this our sins are taken away once we repent and we may be reconciled to God. Come the end of our life we will stand and be judged by the all-pervasive presence of God but we will have confidence through Christ that our lives, offered and lived for Him, will be saved and we may enter heaven."

"Saying, Blessed are they whose iniquities are forgiven, and whose sins are covered. Blessed is the man to whom the Lord will not impute sin."
> \- Romans 4:7-8 KJV.

"For it is written, As I live, saith the Lord, every knee shall bow to me, and every tongue shall confess to God. So then every one of us shall give account of himself to God."
> \- Romans 14:11-12 KJV.

At that moment Mini bent down to pick up more bricks and his back suddenly went pop and he could not move but was in severe pain. It may seem that I was off on one, like a maniac preacher. But there are two things to consider: Firstly John had been making light of God. To me that is like a child making jokes about putting a fork into an electrical socket. There are times for drawing diagrams and explaining about electricity, and there are times for simply shouting "No! You will die!" I have no idea what will happen to me next, or where I could be, or if I will be moved to a different site on Monday. To me it was important to seize the moment and explain these vital things to John. Second, I was about to go off-site for the weekend but this had delayed me right to the point when Mini's back gave out. This seemed to me an appropriate build up to this important event to pray about the issue. Big words about God can only be followed up by the big actions of God.

> *"And they departed, and went through the towns, preaching the gospel, and healing every where."*
>
> - Luke 9:6 KJV.

With that I asked Mini if he wanted me to pray for healing for his back. He said yes.

So there we were. I had just told them, at great length, the Gospel and now I have to pray for a miracle healing. As I started the prayer for Mini I thanked God for the opportunity to talk to John and Mini, and then asked in Jesus' name for Mini to be healed. Mini took a deep breath then said "I felt something go right through me, I have no idea what it was but I can feel that my back is healed." And he carried on working, without thinking about the miracle of that healing or saying any thanks to God.

As things seemed to have reached a natural conclusion I set off on the journey for my daughter and offering my own praise to God for what had happened, for who He is, for doing some good with my life. Rachel, my Mum and I had a wonderful weekend.

Spreading The Word At Work Now Banned

Back at work on Monday morning my boss and the site manager came in to where I was working and told me I had to stop preaching the Gospel. I responded that the people with whom I had spoken had always initiated each conversation and if they do, then I cannot keep silence. "People ask me questions about the meaning and purpose of life and what happens when we die. I have to tell them the truth because it is the truth that extends beyond death." The two men started to walk away, then stopped and the big boss said "News of your preaching has gone as far as head office." Personally I thought that this was great. Having been a Christian for five years I have tried to serve God through the people around me and keep faith in Him.

Jesus had a ministry that only lasted three and a half years on earth, but did innumerable miracles in that time and is now known world-wide as He who rose from the dead.

> *"Jesus answered and said unto them, Destroy this temple, and in three days I will raise it up."*
>
> - John 2:18 KJV.

Jesus was referring to His own body as the temple of God, and that it would come back to life three days after death. Forty days thereafter He ascended into heaven back to the Father. Then the Holy Spirit came into the world and enters the lives of all believers at baptism. As Jesus was raised from the dead we also will be raised from the dead, if we believe and live lives that are dedicated to God. Praise be to God the Father, God the Son and God the Holy Spirit.

The Healing Of Simon

A week later a new carpenter started on site, his name was Simon. He carried his tools into the house upon which he was working and it was clear that his back was giving him problems. I went to meet him and help him to carry his tools and sat with him at break times. We chatted about all manner of things. Eventually I asked Simon if he believed in God, he said "I do and I don't. I am sitting on the fence." And that was the end of that conversation.

Another time I was working and he came across to me. He said "You know what, you need a good woman." I was quite surprised and put down my tools and said "I don't. One blessing from God compensates for all the women in the world. Women certainly are great, but when God blesses you it is beautiful and you want more and more. You can feel rivers of living waters flow through you nourishing you." Simon was the type of guy who had good eye contact and if you didn't look at him whilst you were talking he would tap you on the arm. As we were talking Mini came running up the stairs to find me. I pointed him out to Simon and told the story of the other day when I prayed for him and God healed him on the spot.

Mini said "I have to admit that my back went and Roy prayed for it. I don't know if it was God or whatever but I felt something go through me and totally heal my back." And Mini went on his way without saying why he wanted to see me. With that Simon looked at me with that great eye contact of his and said "I'm going to tell you something now, I have been suffering with a bad back for several years. If what you have told me is true, pray for me, and for God to heal me. I have heard that you have been told to stop preaching the Gospel, I know that, but if God heals me today I will go around the site and tell everyone that God has healed me. Plus I will tell the two bosses what God has done."

Once again I was put on the spot. As you know I like to wait for God's timing and guidance, and this was outside of my comfort zone. Was it outside of my faith? The Bible advises us not to put God to the test, but here I am on the spot. What if I say no? Then all I have preached will look like bluster. Time to put up or shut up. I know that God is real and answers prayers and has a great track record of healing people. All I can do is ask, it is up to God to deliver. I said "OK Simon, come here, God is going to heal your back." Simon was a big guy at 6'3" and a ruddy complexion. I am not a tall man. I put my hand on his back and started the prayer. I thanked God for him, I called upon the name of Jesus Christ and asked God to heal him; then said to Simon to receive the healing remembering what Jesus has done on the Cross. As I was praying Simon started to wobble back and forth and I thought he was going down. I continued the prayer and all of a sudden he shouted out something and it took me completely by surprise so I didn't catch what he said. Then he said "I will let you know" and he went straight back to work.

Around five minutes later he came back and said "That is amazing. The pain has completely gone. God has healed my back." I said "Did you expect any less? Tell me again what are you trying to say." "God had just healed my back." I had, in fact, heard him the first time, but I wanted him to tell me again. I praised Father, Son and Holy Spirit. Simon continued that he was a man of his word and he would be going around the site to tell everyone, including the two bosses, what God had done for him.

Simon did actually go to the bosses cabin and asked them "Why have you told Roy to stop preaching the Gospel?" "Because it offends people." "Listen, Roy just prayed for my back and God healed it." "You are joking." "No I am not, I am telling you that God has just healed my back." From that time on Simon used to preach the Gospel on the site as well as me.

The Healing Of Paul

As time went on the topic of discussion all over the site at most times was the excitement with the goodness of a wonderful God. Paul the painter came to see me and said "I have heard what God is doing on this site and I have heard from them both about the healings of Mini and Simon's backs." Paul was walking with a limp and slightly sideways. "Will you pray for my back?" I said that I would but asked if Paul believed in Jesus, that Jesus was here on earth, that Jesus died on the Cross, that He was buried in a tomb and that after three days He was raised from the dead. Did Paul believe this? He said "I don't know, I will see you later." And he left without having been prayed for. I asked that God would open his eyes and ears to the message of the Gospel and that Paul would find his way back for that healing. This time I was able to ask that it be in God's timing, not mine.

Around lunch time God spoke and told me that it was time to go and pray for Paul. I found him talking with John (who had been up the scaffold with Mini). I asked Paul if he wanted prayer for his back and he said that he really did want it. Before I started the prayer John said "Are we going to see a miracle?" I turned to John and said "You might do, but that is up to God. But I believe that you will."

I put my hand on Paul's back and started to pray for him. I thanked God for him and for John and for all that God was doing in my life. I praised the beauty of His name and finally, in the name of Jesus, asked God to heal Paul.

After the end of the prayer Paul was standing there for a moment, then he said "I don't believe it, that feels beautiful. My back is red hot." At that moment one of the two bosses walked in and Paul said to him and to John "My back is a whole lot better."

He then returned to work and was talking about what had happened for the rest of the day.

A lot of people do not believe in prayer, but they are always quick to put in requests to see if it works. When Jesus was walking the earth and performing thousands of miracles the purpose was to let the people understand who He was. Then they would understand His purpose and that Christ was the one and only Saviour.

> *"And I, if I be lifted up from the earth, will draw all men unto me."*
>
> - John 12:32 KJV.

When Jesus was here on earth He was physically only in one place at a time. After His ascension to heaven He is seated at the right hand of the Father, and can be anywhere and everywhere, the same as the Holy Spirit. As God is not part of creation, He is not subject to its limitations.

> *"Not that any man has seen the Father, save he which is of God, he has seen the Father."*
>
> - John 6:46 KJV.

Today Jesus is alive and active through all believers according to their abilities and healing people through them.

Now at work the topic of conversation seemed always to be God and how He cannot be denied. Each lunch time we would meet in the canteen and have our food whilst they quizzed me about life and why we are here on earth. Being in the public spotlight, even only on a building site, is a great incentive to serve and be faithful to God.

One day, whilst working, Simon came up the ladder to find me. He was moving very slow and his face was a portrait of pain. He said that it was his knees and that they had been worsening over the last week. In the past when they have been that bad he had had to take a fortnight off work. Simon wanted his knees prayed for. I said yes and that I would see him in a minute. Simon clambered back down the ladder giving me time to talk with God. I thanked Him for the many blessings that He had given to me and for use He was making of me. I asked for direction and guidance and timing concerning when would be the right time to pray for Simon. I continued working for another two hours before the loud clear voice of God said "Go and pray for Simon now." So I put down my tools and went to find him. Entering the house that Simon was working on Paul the painter walked in at the same time. The same Paul as above who had had his back healed. Simon asked if Paul could watch. I said that I didn't mind, three hundred people could watch, if they wanted to.

I knelt in front of Simon and put my hands on his knees and prayed. I gave God the glory and thanked Him for blessing me and using me and thanked Him for the blessings that He had given me and thanked Him again for Simon and Paul and then asked God to heal Simon's knees, in the name and power of Christ.

Simon said "That feels incredible, before your prayer all the pain was on the side of the knee and now the pain has gone into the kneecap. He pulled up his trousers to show me his knees and we could all three of us see that his knee caps were red raw and swollen like balloons.

The next day Simon came to see me. He said "You should not be here." I said "Pardon, what do you mean?" Simon said "Look at my knees, the swelling is completely gone. You should not be here, you should be out in full time ministry." I said "I am serving God here and believe that this is where God wants me. Before I came to this site I asked that God would use the opportunity for a blessing."

Dear Reader. Let God into your life, let God transform your life. Come to God and work for your inheritance in heaven. Step out in faith in Christ and ask for God's blessings.

> *"But without faith it is impossible to please Him: for he that comes to God must believe that He is, and that He is a rewarder of them that diligently seek Him."*
> - Hebrews 11:6 KJV.

We can make many mistakes in this life, but it is the hope of salvation through Jesus Christ that will make us enter heaven. We have to believe in Christ, but we also have to live the life that we say that we believe. The works are the fruit of the seed of faith.

Would you say that you are living your life according to God or by your own rules? We might go to Church on Sunday and join in the prayers but is it affecting us deep down? Is it habit or faith? Do we pray in earnestness to God or do we have an eye on how devout we look to others? Further, we cannot be Christians alone, we need to be in God's Church for support and guidance.

One Sunday the pastor asked if I would encourage the congregation with a testimony each week for a month or so, and after I had finished I always asked the people if they had anything to share, but no one ever volunteered. After the service people would be polite and thank me for my story. Once I spoke to a good friend who appeared to be a major player, well, I thought she was. I asked how she was doing in her service to God. She looked away and said "I am not. I haven't done anything for God for ages." Then she walked away with her head low. Looks can be deceiving, we can all say that we love God, but the facts are: how much do we love Him, and how do we love Him? How far are we prepared to go out of our comfortable lives for our Saviour and God? Thinking about the lifelong service given to Christ by His Holy Mother and all of the saints down through the ages, their lives are full to bursting with no regret for losing their part in the world, but only happiness for finding their places doing God's will. Only you know if you have lived the truth of Jesus and dedicated your life to Him and received the Holy Spirit of righteousness, because this is the only righteousness that there is. There is no way to heaven apart from through Christ.

> *"And we have all become like unclean people; all our righteousness is like the rag of a menstruating woman."*
> - Isaiah 64:6 LXX.

We need to be put right with God through repentance and the forgiveness of our sins. We need to dedicate ourselves to God, then live out a life that reflects that if we wish to enter heaven and eternal life after our own death. It is our wilfulness that is the barrier between ourselves and God.

> *"But seek you first the kingdom of God, and His righteousness; and all these things shall be added unto you."*
> — Matthew 6:33 KJV.

Let us take stock, do you have what it takes to enter heaven? Do you have the seed of life and assurance within that you will be saved when you appear before God?

Dear Reader, I am preaching hard here, straight to you, and it may come across as too strong, relentless or needlessly aggressive. But what can I say? Eternal life is surely so much more important than anything temporary in this world. In this life everything that we value ages, rusts, deteriorates, fades away. Nothing lasts for ever, in fact it is shocking how short a life span stuff and things have. Sometimes I feel that I have to shout to help people look up from their rotting possessions and to think about the life that we are promised after death. It is there if we want it, if we give ourselves to Christ and then spend the rest of our lives working for it. Of course it is a terrifying thought to give up control of our own lives, and it takes years of practice, as you have seen in my stories.

> *"Come unto me, all you that labour and are heavy laden, and I will give you rest. Take my yoke upon you, and learn of me; for I am meek and lowly in heart: and you shall find rest unto your souls. For my yoke is easy, and my burden is light."*
> — Matthew 11:28-30 KJV.

Here Christ is telling us that trying to do it alone is a back breaking exercise. Joining forces with God allows Him to carry your sorrows and for you to rest. In return He offers you employment with Him, Who is the most humble being in existence. The work that He gives is surprisingly easy. For example it appears to me that my job is to tell people the Gospel. So I have to talk to people? For me that is an easy task and I am happy for it to fill my life. Other people are called to other tasks, some of which are tucked away and done alone.

One day we will die, we can all agree with that, no matter how much we try to ignore it. How long will you live? God knows everything including when, where and how you will die. After the death of our bodies our spirit lives on until the final resurrection and the joining together with our renewed, fixed and eternal bodies. Ours, but better. Can we take out insurance against this? Can we put in place a pension for after death? No, of course not. But God offers us accommodation in heaven, whatever nourishment that will be required will come straight from Him.

> *"For God so loved the world, that he gave His only begotten Son, that whosoever believes in Him should not perish, but have everlasting life."*
> - John 3:16 KJV.

What is more, once our lives are in God's service all these benefits are free. If you have given your life to God then you have nothing left. All that you have is His and letting go is so sweet. We clasp our paltry treasures, gripping their rotting remains to our chests. To let go, to say "Here God, please use these temporary things that I have, my house, my car, my possessions"; this brings such a fantastic feeling of being able to let go. God certainly does not require all of us to be poor, but He does expect us to help each other.

My walk with Christ continues and every day I discover my mistakes and ask God to help me to rectify them, then to become more aware and more thankful. His blessings overwhelm me. Even a brand new car can break down, but the manufacturers do not send angels to help you. I look back on my life with God and thank Him for being amazing. Some parts of it may seem like a dream but I am telling the truth. There have been many times when I have broken down in tears and cried out to God for less of me and more of Him. It is all about faith and trust in God. To rely on Him, to have a rewarding and active prayer life and to take the time to listen for the quiet voice of God and then to want to act on it.

> *"The just shall live by faith."*
> - Romans 1:17 KJV.

There is a huge difference between faith and belief. Belief is simply accepting that something exists without having proof. I accept that Australia exists though I have never been there. Plenty of people have talked about it and I have seen pictures that do not appear to be faked. I simply accept in belief.

Faith is the utter reliance upon something even though we don't know how it works. For example I have faith in my car. I have no idea how many parts there are in it, or what most of them do. I understand bits of it, but have no clear idea of how all of those hundreds of moving parts make it move. I just sit in and turn the key and it takes me where I want to go. I also know that it may break down and one day will be useless.

I have faith in God. I can ask Him for healings for people. I can pray. I have confidence that He will answer in His own way and own time. This is faith in God. I utterly trust in Him, even though I have no idea how it all works. As God is eternal I also know that he will never break down and never be useless. So we need to learn faith in God that He will look after us each day, feed us, clothe us, direct and guide us.

A Prayer

- Have mercy, Lord, on our spiritual fathers, mothers, brothers, sisters and children, and save them, and by their holy prayers forgive us our transgressions.

Les And The Bike Accident

Remember Les? He was an alcoholic, had a back with five vertebrae missing and asked me to pray for his broken hand on his doorstep. He came to tell me that he had been knocked off his bicycle by a bus and that it had hurt his back. He rang the bus company to inform them of the incident. They kindly replied with a letter apologising and accepting responsibility. At the hospital the doctor examined him for his insurance claim. When I saw him he was in a lot of pain and using painkillers. He said that he would be taking the bus company to court for compensation. I asked if he wanted healing for his back but Les said no, if he had to go to court and looked fine it would undermine his claim and he didn't want to lie in court by faking pain.

A couple of days later I went to see Les, letting myself in with the key that he had previously given me. He was sitting in quiet contemplation in the lounge. He said "I have been thinking about what you said about praying for me. It seems that I have turned down the offer of a blessing by God. I have been greedy in looking ahead to the compensation money, but I should have been looking to God for healing. Will you pray for God to heal my back? If there is any compensation money then that is up to God." I said that this was good news. It was not for me to say anything about his decision even though I personally felt that it was wrong to have prayed for him when he didn't want me to and his heart was not in the right place.

So we prayed there and then, giving praise and thanks to God. Les asked God to forgive him for being blinded by the thought of money and making the wrong decision. He said that he should have put God first. For the second time God healed Les' back. God has always loved us and always will. God has always healed those who ask in faith, and always will.

> "Jesus Christ the same yesterday, and today, and for ever."
> - Hebrews 13:8 KJV.

From that moment Les did not need the painkillers and set about repairing his bike. It is too easy to look to the visible doctors and pills for relief and healing than to remember the invisible God and His infinite resources of instantaneous healing. God is able to distribute His infinite powers as and when needed by His believers, His Mother and His saints. Wherever you put your last word is where you put your faith.

My Mum's Video
For those first eight years of being a Christian I spent a lot of time driving up and down the M5 and M4 to see my daughter and my Mum. Mum loved seeing the both of us and it filled me with happiness to be with the both of them. On one visit Mum said that she was now falling out of bed, even when she sleeps in the middle she somehow manages to find the floor. I asked if I would be allowed to pray for her that God would protect her from further falls. She agreed so I started the prayer. I asked that God would keep angels by her side to protect her and make her safe and free from harm. After the prayer Mum said that she already felt

My Walk With Jesus

much better.

When we let God into a situation we are basically confessing that we need help and passing the whole burden onto God. As God made everything, anything that seems heavy to us is of little load to Him. We acknowledge that our efforts are unsuccessful and that God will do better. Be confident God will take care of it all as you hand it to Him in prayer. Then simply wait in faith for the results. God provides answers that are a) better than we think and b) later than we think.

The Monday after that weekend with Mum she rang me to say what had happened. "On Sunday night I was in bed and it was like someone lying on either side of me, stopping me from falling out." My sister Linda suggested that it was the spirit of my Dad however I believe that it was an exact answer to prayer and that indeed God's angels were keeping guard. Mum never fell out of bed again showing to me that God's angels were always on duty.

Mum loved our visits and she also loved coming to stay with me as we could spend time together and she liked being by the sea. Once Mum stayed with me for six months whilst my nephew Steve was her house-sitter. When Mum eventually went home she found that the video player was not working so she asked me to have a look at it. I fiddled with it for an hour or so, with no success. The next day Mum and I were seated watching TV in each other's company when she asked me to try the video again. Even though the previous day I had only managed to fetch fuzzy black lines from it she said "Give it one more go, because miracles do happen." Of course I could not say no to my Mum and thought "Yes, miracles do happen if you have faith. And nothing is too small for God."

Yes miracles do happen but once again I felt conflicted. On the one hand the old command not to tempt God, and it sometimes feels that asking the Almighty Creator about little things is to tempt Him. He might roar from heaven "I am the Alpha and Omega, I am the creator of life, and you want me to fix your VHS?" On the other hand He loves us all dearly and to withhold even the minutiae of our lives from Him is to carve out an area where He is not welcome.

So I knelt down on the floor in front of the video player and turned it on. As the previous night the TV showed only fuzzy black lines. I was reaching out my hand to the unit and suddenly a picture appeared on the screen in full colour. Upon examination we found that all five channels were working and also the video cassette part. I turned to Mum and said "Yes, miracles do happen." This is clearly a little thing, the VHS of an old lady works again, but for me it was part of my training to totally rely on God. I must give over all the little things to God until He has all of my life. Hold nothing back.

For all of us, at some point in our lives strange things happen which cannot be explained. Why would my Mum ask me to give it one more go and then say that miracles do happen? Was it because the first time that I tried to repair it I was relying on my own skills and once again forgetting to give it to God? God loves to be involved in all that we do, no matter how big or small. I cannot work miracles, but I know someone Who can and I believe with all of my heart that God prompted Mum to speak those words so that the door to heaven might open just a crack so that she could see through and He could call to her. I was only a bit part actor in this, my Mum's story. As such I didn't see the beginning, though it was my heart's desire that I would know that she had been drawn to God and started a new life with Christ.

Mum would always take an interest in what God was doing in my life and loved to hear the stories from work that you have now read. This was the first time that she had seen anything like that, about what God will do in return for faith. Only the heaven-sent can do miracles and perform healings. Things happen for a reason and God will always bring good out of bad. Usually we don't see the full picture but just trust in Him to bring us through.

Pain In My Knees

There was a time when I used to play a lot of five-a-side football and have accumulated a lot of damage to both knees. Both knees were permanently inflamed, stiff and gave me a lot of pain. Walking was difficult, it was troublesome to try to get into the car, it could take five minutes to exit the car by heaving on the door and of course I couldn't go to work. I don't like taking painkillers as I think that I should trust in God for healing, allowing that God also heals through doctors. At that time I was rethinking my policy about painkillers. I prayed many times for God to heal my knees but nothing happened. Perhaps God wants me to use the other route, so I went to the doctor who gave me painkillers but didn't tell me what was the problem. I kept going back until he referred me for a scan at Bristol hospital. A scan is not a pleasant experience as one must lie motionless in the tunnel of the machine for three quarters of an hour. The surgeon looked at the results and said that they needed to operate soon. Then he said "I'll tell you what, I will give you an open appointment and when your knees are too bad to move, come in and we will do both operations." And there we left it.

After that my knees continued to deteriorate but I still wanted God to do the healing. Perhaps it is easier to trust Him with big things than little things. As I couldn't work I decided to go to Mum for a week, as you know a three hour journey. Upon arrival the pain was excruciating and I could barely walk into the house. On that Sunday I went to worship with a local group that I knew and the pastor was on form talking about forgiveness and healing. He said that when he had finished preaching we will do a service of healing for anyone who needs prayer, but suddenly he said that it was time to stop preaching and immediately start the healing service. There was a team up front and they indicated that people should come forward. With some difficulty I managed to walk to the front and stood before a lady who asked for what was it that I required prayer. I told her about my knees over the past year, the hospital scan, the open appointment. I also told her that my preference was for God to do the healing and I believe that He can and that He wants to.

The lady started her prayer but quickly stopped. She said "God has instructed me to stop as He says that at some time in your life you were brought to your knees?" I said that yes about a year ago that my wife had decided to end our marriage and I lost my children, all the money, the money intended for the tax man, the car and a good chunk of the house and since then have to also pay maintenance. In this way I was certainly brought to my knees. The lady said "God says: have you forgiven her?" I said that yes I had, and one better I would have her back today. This was all too emotional for me and tears were running down my face. She restarted the prayer but God interrupted her a third time to tell her that "From this moment on your knees are going to be healed."

As soon as she said the word "healed" both of my knees felt like fire and by the time I had completed the short walk back to my seat the knees felt fine and I had a look to see that the swelling had totally gone down and the legs were pain-free. I put my head in my hands in wonder at what had happened and took the time to praise God for His goodness to me. The congregation started singing a hymn that was new to me "At The Name Of Jesus", and have never heard again. The Bible reference that formed the basis of the words was whispered to me by that heavenly voice:

> *"And began to salute him, Hail, King of the Jews! And they smote him on the head with a reed, and did spit upon him, and bowing their knees worshipped him."*
> - Mark 15:18 KJV.

All the levels of what was happening were revolving around me: the pain in the knees being somehow linked to an emotional matter around my marriage and a spiritual connection about forgiveness. The new hymn including a mention of knees, the whispering of the reference to really help to hammer the message home. The realisation that I had spent most of my life with my back to God doing things my way. Look where I had ended up: in divorce court. But the truth is that God knows all about you, He even knows how many hairs are on your head. He knows what you are about to do before you do it, yet He will not interfere with our free will. As I have mentioned before; I believe that suffering is God's telephone call to us, to help us to exhaust other options so that we will find ourselves eventually wanting to turn to Him.

I was brought to my knees both physically and metaphorically, but God in His goodness picked me up. If God is for you, who can be against you?

Mum The Christian

After the service I returned to Mum. She was amazed by the story and we both had a good look at my now normal knees. A bit later I decided to go home so that I could work and bring in some money. I said goodbye to Mum in the kitchen. Her normal practice was to follow me outside to the car to wave me on my way, but this time I found myself behind the wheel alone. As she

My Walk With Jesus

didn't come outside I started the engine and put the car into gear. I was just about to drive away when the heavenly voice said "Go back to your Mum, she wants to give her life to Jesus." So I locked the car and went back inside. Mum was still standing in the kitchen with her back to the sink so I walked up to her, took her hands and asked how she felt about giving her life to Jesus? She said that she had been meaning to do it for ages but didn't know how. So right there and then I led her in a prayer to Jesus Christ repenting of her sins, asking for forgiveness and vowing her life to Him.

Suddenly Mum said "That's amazing. During the prayer I felt the weight of my sins lift off me." Praise be to God. It repeated the lesson for me that when God tells you to do something, do it right away. Don't miss the blessing that God has lined up. After an hour with Mum it was time for me to go home with two new knees, a Mum who was now a Christian and partaking of God's kingdom. That is a top weekend, thanks to God for blessing both of us.

Bye Sandra, Enjoy Birmingham

Two weeks later I was with my home worship group and after the service was talking with a disabled family who were living in rented accommodation and had decided to move to Birmingham. I wondered if they might need help with the move, or any fixes in the current house so that they could have their full deposit back. They didn't have a lot of money, and every penny can help during a move. Whilst chatting I noticed a lump on the head of Sandra, but did not say anything. Sandra said "Do you know of a carpenter who can repair kitchen drawers?" I told her that that was my job and that I would be happy to do that.

There were several reasons for their upcoming move, she said, and the lump on her head was one of them. Apparently it was cancer, she was receiving treatment, but the lump wasn't responding. She was due at the hospital the next day and was hoping that they would be able to do something about it. She was worried. I offered to pray for her and she accepted. After the prayer I said that I would be round the next day for the drawers, ringing first.

On Monday Les and I went round. Sandra had great news and I could see that the lump was smaller. She said that there was no pain in her head. As she was due back in hospital for more tests later that week we had more time for prayer before I took away the drawers for repair.

Two days later I went there again and Sandra had even more good news. The lump had completely vanished and there was still no pain and furthermore the hospital had given her the all-clear from cancer.

Sandra's daughter Brenda came into the house. She was a shy girl and quiet. Before Sandra could tell her the good news Brenda said "When you prayed for my Mum on Sunday I had a vision. I saw fire coming from heaven onto Mum's head." Sandra told Brenda the good news. All of us were crying with happiness and offering thanks and praise to God.

Sandra then shared some stories with me. One was concerning Brenda when she was six years old. Her legs were different diameters, one fat, one skeletal. Brenda one day said "I am going to pray to Jesus and ask Him to make both of my legs the same size." Sandra showed me a photograph of Brenda at six with the odd sized legs. Christ did heal her legs to a perfect match. God is so generous to give what we ask, if asked in faith. When you have prayed then believe that it will come to pass and wait in confidence for the miracle – you will be amazed.

Brenda And A Bag Of Coal

Sandra told another story about when they had no money or food or coal and food would appear on her doorstep. On a cold day Brenda said "I am going to ask Jesus to send us some coal. The next day the coal man came with a delivery. I pointed out that we had not placed an order, nor had any money. He answered 'The coal has been paid for, open up your coal shed.' Well we praised the Lord as He is our provider."

A month after this Sandra, Brenda and Derek moved up to Birmingham with the help of several parishioners.

As time went on I continued to serve the Lord in any opportunity that I spotted. Perhaps putting away the chairs after a service or painting the parish or giving people lifts. I just wanted to try to give God something back for all that He had given me. We all have gifts and God wants us to use these gifts in His service, by helping others. That is a form of worship to our

Saviour and God and we are using what He has given us responsibly.

At the final judgement the light of Christ will shine through us and show us the bad things that we have done, even the corners of ourselves that we didn't know were sinful. If we still want Christ then we will be rewarded with eternal life in His eternal presence. I love to find ways to serve God and little chances always present themselves. Then the challenge of listening for God's still small voice.

The Healing Of Martin

One Sunday Terry Pike was preaching on forgiveness and healing. I was listening to Terry but also noticed a young man three rows in front with his head in his hands and leaning forward. Terry then called this young man to the front to share his conversion story, and this he did, but then went straight back to his seat and resumed the same position, now rocking backwards and forwards. I didn't know him, but it seemed to me like he needed help. Then the heavenly voice spoke and said "After the service fetch Mike and I want you both to pray for him." This I did. It transpired that Mike knew him and his name was Martin.

We stood in a huddle with me in the middle and with an arm around each of their shoulders. We prayed and as we did so Martin began to shake and when we finished praying he stopped shaking and just stood there with his head down. He said "That was amazing. Your hand was red hot on my neck. I was healed of epilepsy but it left me with a bad neck for years. But I can tell you that God has healed my neck."

The three of us were standing together praising God. One thing is for sure; if God tells you to do something, be bold and do it. God wants to bless you and strengthen that relationship that you have with Him.

The Healing Of Tracey

A couple of weeks later I was in a different place and the pastor asked if I would like to share some testimonies. After the service a woman with whom I was an acquaintance, called Tracey, came up to me and we talked. She said "You under estimate what God is going to do in your life." I thought that that was a really strange statement, but she went on to explain herself. She told me that she had had a bad leg for many a month and that many people had prayed for her, but the expected healing did not occur. She said that as she was simply talking with me she could feel God healing her leg right there and then. By the time that we finished talking she looked and said that the leg was completely healed. I was astonished and grappling with the idea that God would work through me without me needing to pray. It put me in mind of the Apostle Peter.

> *"Insomuch that they brought forth the sick into the streets, and laid them on beds and couches, that at the least the shadow of Peter passing by might overshadow some of them. There came also a multitude out of the cities round about unto Jerusalem, bringing sick folks, and them which were vexed with unclean spirits: and they were healed every one."*
> - Acts 5:15-16 KJV.

I understand this to be a confirmation of what God is able to do in one's life and will do if you walk with Him.

Terry was the pastor here and I went to tell him what had happened for Tracey and her leg. He said that he had been one of those who had prayed for her without any resultant healing.

God knows the heart of man and you cannot deceive Him. He knows whether or not one is truly for Him, love Him and desire to serve Him. However the closer one arises to God the more one is attacked. God allows some attacks in order to strengthen our faith, but by trusting in Him one may always be brought through.

My ex-wife Amanda had become quite the atheist and suggested to my daughter Rachel that I loved God more than her. When Rachel later asked me I was left speechless. Then the heavenly voice provided the words that I repeated to Rachel: "By loving God I can love you more." She appreciated this and smiled and the expression on her face made it clear that she thought this an acceptable answer. I believe that these words were provided to me, and were exactly what Rachel wanted to hear. For two reasons, first because God is love and second because I am not sharp enough to think of something like that on the spot.

We had another lovely weekend making a doll's house and I helped her to decorate it.

Andy The Tacker

The next week at work I was on a new site called Elmborough Gardens. Andy the plasterboard tacker and I were working on the same house. He was in pain and finding it hard to do his job. Andy was always blunt with his opinions, an unbeliever, and liked one-upmanship. Sadly for Him God is bigger, cleverer and stronger. He and I had had many a good sparring conversation, but today he was quiet with pain and needed help. I had already told Andy many times that God is the only healer and it must have sunk in as Andy asked for prayer. I agreed that I would, but you know my methods – wait for the prompting of God. Ten minutes later Andy asked again and I assured him that I would do. Both times I carried on working and was in silent prayer about the matter, presenting the situation for God's consideration and asking Him for guidance about the matter.

The heavenly voice prompted that it was time and to find Andy right now. As I went Andy was searching for me and said "Please pray for me, my back is badly hurting." I asked Andy "Do you want me to pray for you right now, and ask God to heal your back?" He said that it had been bad for a week. As he said this he was leaning on the wall with one hand braced on his hip and he was looking away. I put one hand on his back and started the prayer. I praised Jesus and thanked God for Andy, and asked God to touch Andy with His healing and to heal him in Jesus' name.

After the prayer Andy stayed in that position for two minutes. Andy was exactly the sort of guy to enjoy telling you that something didn't work without pulling any punches, but he remained motionless. Eventually he turned to look at me and said "I will let you know." He smiled and walked away without the limp and certainly not appearing to be in pain any more. Inside I knew that God had healed him because there is no other God besides my God and He is life.

The next day Andy found me on site and came running up the stairs, so I mentioned this and asked after his back. He said "As a matter of fact it is fine, thank you." And then he left.

So many people are quick to put in their prayer requests out of curiosity to see if they work as they have nothing to lose. When God heals them they rationalise it and deny the miracle. God is not in the habit of throwing miracles all over the place, each one is a personal gift to that person and intended to strengthen, or start, their relationship with Him.

> *"O taste and see that the Lord is good."*
> - Psalms 33:9 LXX.

Two thousand years ago Christ God joined Himself with mankind, in the person of Jesus, in the womb of His Holy Mother. As Jesus Christ He walked Israel using miracles to draw the attention of the nation to the incarnation of God, laying out the scriptures regarding the Saviour to be sent by God and making it abundantly clear that in Him all these things came true.

> *"For the invisible things of Him from the creation of the world are clearly seen, being understood by the things that are made, even His eternal power and Godhead; so that they are without excuse:"*
> - Romans 1:20 KJV.

God the Creator of all sends His Holy Spirit to abide in all those who are baptised into His Apostolic Church. My life stands testimony to this truth. No one can see God the Father and live. We approach Him through the other two persons of the Trinity, God the Holy Spirit, who abides in our hearts, and God the Christ, who abides in His One True Church.

> *"Jesus said unto him, I am the way, the truth, and the life: no man cometh unto the Father, but by me."*
> - John 14:6 KJV .

> *"Believe you not that I am in the Father, and the Father in me? The words that I speak unto you I speak not of myself: but the Father that dwells in me, He does the works. Believe me that I am in the Father,*

and the Father in me: or else believe me for the very works' sake. Verily, verily, I say unto you, He that believes on me, the works that I do shall he do also; and greater works than these shall he do; because I go unto my Father. And whatsoever you shall ask in my name, that will I do, that the Father may be glorified in the Son. If you shall ask any thing in my name, I will do it."

- John 14:10-14 KJV.

If God should speak to you or heal you, don't turn your back. Call out to God and ask Him to take control of your life. Jesus Christ is the Saviour of creation.

Wrong Turning On The M5

It was my Mum's birthday. It was winter, cold, wet, foggy and dark. I was on the M5 and the speed limit was down to 30 miles an hour. Perhaps it was the weather and the visibility being so bad, but I lost my sense of direction and turned off at the wrong junction. Heading down unfamiliar roads I soon became lost. I found myself on an unknown dual carriageway. Passing a layby there was a parked lorry flashing his hazard lights. I pulled in behind him to ask the driver for directions. As soon as I parked the lorry driver was running towards my car and he said "Are you lost?" And he gave me directions back to the motorway and turned and ran back to his lorry and shot off into the thick fog. It seemed to me that he had been waiting there for me, delivered his piece and went on his way. I certainly believe that this is the way it happens with God. He is quite able to talk to people and angels and put them in position for when you need them.

"The Lord shall keep you from all evil, the Lord shall guard your soul. The Lord shall keep your coming in and your going out, from henceforth and for evermore."

- Psalms 120:7-8 LXX.

It always amazes me how God works, how He blesses us and how He guides my steps. And these blessings are for all who want Him.

Could Not Find Kevin's House

At this point in my stories I had only been a Christian for five years, so young in the faith and still learning. I have been told that one of God's gifts to me is to encourage people so I try to do this.

Once my friend Kevin had no work and was upset about it. I promised to pay him a visit one evening. He checked to make sure that I knew where he lived, and I said yes that I did. The following night I set off and, you guessed it, I could not find his house and became lost. There was no one around to ask. I said "Lord, there is always no-one around when you need them." God said "I am always here. Ask for directions in that off-licence."

In the shop I took my place as number two in the queue before a third man joined us. As the first man was busy I turned and asked number three if he knew how to find Brough Road. He didn't know, but number one had completed his business, turned around and said that he knew how to find it, because he lived there. He then asked which house number I was looking for. I told him number three and said that he lived at "number two, follow me". The estate that Kevin lived on had over a thousand houses, so the chances of this being a random meeting were slimmer than slim. Thanks to God for another rescue, for knowing all things and for directing the path of anyone who puts their trust into Him.

My own learning and training with God has shown me that even when I go wrong, which is a regular occurrence, He will put me back on the right road. It is a great journey, exciting and amazing. God is truly my best friend as He looks after me in ways that humans cannot do.

Kevin At Work

Arriving at Kevin's house I shared with him the events of the evening – he was enthralled. It was a wonderful evening. Kevin asked me if there were any jobs on the building site and also he needed prayer, which we did there and then. The next day at work I enquired about any jobs. The site manager said that there were none, but strangely a new labourer would start each day that week. I saw one labourer throw down his shovel and walk out, but still I was told that there were no spare jobs.

That evening I went to see Les and Kevin came up in the chat and the heavenly voice surprised me by saying "Fast for Kevin's situation." I repeated this to Les who offered to fast as well. I said that the matter really seemed for me and Les asked how long am I to fast for? I said that I didn't know, but God would let me know. That night I had a dream. I arose and looked at the clock to find it was 16:00. I started eating and then woke up.

The next day was a bank holiday, but I felt that I should go to work to see the site manager. He asked me if my friend was still looking for a job. I followed him to the site office and from there rang Kevin. The clock in the office said 15:45. Kevin's phone was engaged, but I kept on trying until I finally connected with him at 16:00. I told him about the job, but he said that he had just been offered one as a teacher. I praised God then told him about the dream and the fasting. Kevin was amazed.

It would have been great working alongside each other, but only God can see the big picture and arranges things in ways that we don't understand. The main lesson is to stay faithful and obedient to God at all times, no matter what the signs around us.

Powersaw Powerless

The next day the holiday was over and we were all back at work and I was thankful to God for Kevin's great new job, certainly better than a labourer, and was musing on all these things. I was using a powersaw given to me by Les, old but usable. For this job it was being worked quite hard and the bottom half broke away rendering it, and me, useless. I planned to take it around to Les that night to see if he could repair it as he was a mechanic when younger and had done several similar jobs for me. I went to put the useless saw in the car and, may God be praised, an unexpected and uncalled for little miracle – on the road right by my car was the bottom half of exactly the same saw. That night Les repaired it from both parts in fifteen minutes and that saw served me reliably for decades on. God looked after his worthless servant and provided even before being asked.

Exercising faith in God is to exercise your relationship with Him, and all manner of things start to happen around you. It has given me cause to stop and think many times and changed my whole way of life. God knows all, He is outside time and is not limited, as we are, by past, present and future. He sees all and knows all.

> *"Neither is there any creature that is not manifest in His sight: but all things are naked and opened unto the eyes of Him with whom we have to do."*
> - Hebrews 4:13 KJV.

Unfortunately this means that we are unable to do something wrong and assume that there will be no reckoning. We are accountable for all of our actions. God watches us for all of our lives. God knew our lives complete from ages past, from birth to death.

> *"As for the days of our years, in their span, they be threescore years and ten. And if we be in strength, mayhap fourscore years; and what is more than these is toil and travail. For mildness is come upon us, and we shall be chastened."*
> - Psalms 89:10 LXX.

Seventy or eighty years is not long. Then what? The choice is all yours. I have reached my sixties with only a few hundreds of weekends until I am 70.

> *"So make Your right hand known to me, and to them that in their heart are instructed in wisdom."*
> - Psalms 89:12 LXX.

As you patiently continue to read my stories and hear of my walk with God you see that I choose to involve God in all areas of my life. You will want to know why I do this. It is because of God's love for me and all those many experiences of God at work. Because of Christ's salvific action on the Cross for all of creation, and therefore all of mankind. Because of that action claiming creation back again for God from sin. Because He allows us to repent of our sins and accepts us in love. He has done all the hard work, all He requires of us is faith and an ongoing Christian life.

Some people only want to believe in visible things, this is called empiricism. The normal riposte to that is to point out those things which are not visible: gravity, air, radio signals, how a microwave oven cooks food, electricity and of course, love. All of these things we depend upon in everyday life without knowing how they work. This is faith. In exactly the same way we can depend upon God. As I was, you too will be amazed.

A Prayer

- Have mercy, O Lord, on the old and the young, the needy, the orphans and widows, and all who are in sickness and sorrow, distress and affliction, oppression and captivity, in prison and confinement. Save them, together with Your servants who are under persecution for Your sake and for the sake of the Christian faith. Remember them, visit them, strengthen and comfort them, and by Your power grant them speedy relief, freedom and deliverance.

Tyre Repair

I love to talk with God and involve Him in everything that is happening, even the little things. Once the car had a slow puncture that needed repair. Rather than trying to drive it any great distance I took it to the local garage. As it was my birthday I didn't want to spend the day waiting there. The mechanic informed me of the reasonable price and said that it would take an hour, more time than I wanted to spend on this project on this day, however it was an urgent job, so needs must. As I was waiting God spoke and said to go to another garage nearby. I made my apologies and moved on. The second garage quoted a lower price and half an hour wait.

Thankful to God for these two small improvements I resolved to stay as I had been directed here. However after only one minute of waiting I was called through and this mechanic started the repair and completed it within five minutes. When trying to pay for it using their original quote I was told to forget about it and just give them enough for some tea bags. Later I found that he had overpaid the change, so I went back there to rectify the situation. God sees all. However my thanks to God were fulsome for addressing even this tiny problem in my life with such alacrity and efficiency.

The Pearl Of Great Price

"Again, the kingdom of heaven is like unto a merchant man, seeking goodly pearls: Who, when he had found one pearl of great price, went and sold all that he had, and bought it."
- Matthew 13:45-46 KJV.

Cold Car Requires Repair

Cars come, cars go. My trade covers a lot of ground and I always need a car. It is Christmas 1999 at my Mum's and my car is stolen. This is now the third time and each time is a shock. There were no valuables or tools in it, only my favourite sticker in the rear window "Carpenter from Nazareth seeks joiners". As I am a carpenter I enjoyed that sticker. The police quickly found the trashed remains of the car, now useless. More sad, to me, the sticker is gone.

Due to go to work in two days the search for a new car is on. We find one in the paper, book a viewing at the end of the next day. We view, we like, we buy.

On the 160 mile drive home I quickly find that the heater does not work. At home I book into the main dealer for a service whilst a friend runs me to the building site.

The dealer phones to say that they have replaced the heater matrix, at a great price. I am not happy, but arrange to pick it up the next day. One hour later the dealer phones again to say that the water pump is broken and this will cost hundreds more. The next day, at the dealer, my car is not to be seen. The manager says that the waterways in the top of the head of the engine are all blocked and so it needs a new top half of the engine. This will cost thousands, but is more than the car cost and is more than I have. He wants me to make a decision to spend the money there and then but I say that I cannot. As the water pump was not to blame he does not charge me for that, and I pay for the first work on the heater matrix and take the car home where it will live on my drive until such time as an answer presents itself.

That afternoon, at home, I had a conversation with God about the matter. It appeared that I might have bought a car already dead and too expensive to repair. I gave the problem to God alongside my inability to find a solution. God's heavenly voice spoke "Ring Mike". Always double check. I asked God who could fix the car and God spoke again "Ring Mike".

"A man's steps are directed by the Lord,
and a mortal - how could he understand
His ways?"
— Proverbs 20:24 LXX.

Then a third time "Ring Mike." So I rang Mike. He was not at work that day. I told him that God told me to ring, even though Mike clearly didn't believe that, and did he know of any good mechanics? He said he only knew one, who worked at the big main dealer that I had just come back from. I rang the number given and spoke to the mechanic who was not at work that day and made an appointment for later that day at his house. He fixed it in five minutes, he simply bled the system and charged me ten pounds.

God is very good to those who ask. This is a small thing to you, but an important part of my life. God does not want you to worry and stress and struggle on your own except for those times when He is training you. God wants you to cast all of your worries on to Him. He sees your future and knows that with His help you can avoid wrong turns and dead ends.

"But seek you first the kingdom of God, and
His righteousness; and all these things
shall be added unto you."
— Matthew 6:33 KJV.

New Car Break Down

As you can imagine over the years I had spent a lot of money on the motorway picking up my daughter and going across Britain to see my Mum. It is reasonable to say that this has been a contributory cause of my many cars failing. This new car was on the motorway and the engine started making a lot of noise. I pulled over onto the hard shoulder and rang for the AA recovery. The car would not start so they put it on the lorry. We took it home and dropped it outside Les' house because he was a mechanic. The AA man suggested that the engine was dead and the car would need a new one. I thought "Here we go again, someone saying that this car needs a fortune spent on it."

The next day Les looked it over and his first thought was the water pump, then the starter motor. Both of these are expensive items. He looked confused, I was confused, so I made my excuses and popped home. Actually I needed to make some space, clear my head and focus on God for the answer. I asked God for someone to provide the clear answer, preferably without costing me a fortune.

The heavenly voice of God spoke loud and clear "Ring Glen." Glen was a mechanic with his own garage. What happened next was verification to me that everything is better off in God's hands. I told Glen the long story of the problem and Glen simply said "It's the alternator. I have an identical model to yours in the garage right now with the same problem. I am actually holding his alternator in my hand right now." How amazing is that? God clearly knew who could provide the answer and arranged the call.

Going back to Les I explained what had happened, we found an alternator and Les put it on and it started first time. Thanks God for fixing my car yet again.

God Tells Me That Leslie's Wife Is Pregnant

Two weeks later Leslie rang. Remember Leslie? This is the one that let me live with him and turned out to be an alcoholic, not Les from across the road. Leslie's life had improved, he had married Wendy and had a child. When Leslie rang, he appeared to be stressed and he wanted to meet. He said he would be round in forty-five minutes. As I went for a wash I wondered what had upset Leslie. The heavenly voice of God spoke and said "Leslie is coming to tell you that his wide Wendy is pregnant." I knew Leslie quite well and knew that he had had a vasectomy after the first child, so the pregnancy was quite a puzzle.

Leslie arrived and drove straight to the point. I told him that God had mentioned it in the last half hour. Leslie sat down amazed.

In the great scheme of things it is hardly surprising that the

Creator of all things would know about the pregnancy. Why He would tell me ahead of Leslie's arrival is only for God to know.

The rest of the story about Leslie, Wendy and the pregnancy is not my story, and not mine to tell.

God Wants Me To Share Testimonies

It is now the year 2000 and it feels to me that God wants me to share these testimonies with other Christians. I mentioned this to Mum as we walked through the town of Dunstable together.

A Lady Approaches Me To Come To Her Group

Minutes later a beautiful black lady approached us to give us a leaflet which said "Come to our church and tell us what God is doing in your life." As we were talking about this very subject Mum and I agreed that this is an opening and we smiled at each other.

Brother-In-Law Asks Me To Talk At A Prayer Meeting

Back at Mum's house brother-in-law Mike popped in to ask if I would come to his prayer meeting that very night to give my testimonies. Even someone as thick as I can recognise God driving a point home. In the space of one hour the subject has come up three times with two solid invitations.

Go To Give Testimony

The prayer meeting that night was a source of inspiration for me. Mike led the prayers and played guitar. He introduced me and I stood to tell my stories. Someone stood up and said that he wanted some of those experiences. Many people came at the end to request prayer for all kinds of issues.

At this point I had been a Christian for seven years, always learning to lean on God more. I served Him when I was able to see the opportunities. I do not know why God had chosen me to witness so many miracles and healings and why He gives me blessings over the smallest of things, except because He wanted to. He does not love me more than anyone else and equally distributes His love to us all. Those who have faith will ask for more and see more.

The next morning I went to St Hugh's, local to Mum's house, and wondered if I would be called upon to share the story of my knees from a year ago. I drove completely absent-mindedly and somehow ended up at a little place in Luton. Wonder upon wonder it was the Gospel group of the black lady with the leaflet. I was the only white man in the place, but they made me feel so welcome. I felt like they were waiting for me, as I go on you will see why.

The service started at 10:30 and ended at 16:00 and I enjoyed every minute of it. At midday the pastor said that it was testimony time and he wanted each and every one of us to share what God is doing in your life. He allocated forty-five minutes. I had no idea to where I was driving or that the pastor would say that. However every time someone finished another would run to the front before I could. Out of all the stories shared there was no real evidence of God's power. Some read from the Bible, some would say something nice about God. As person after person rushed to the front I wondered if I would have to crash my way to the front to put in a word or two. However God always knows everything. With ten minutes to go and no sign of any slowing of the people who wanted to talk, I finally relaxed and gave my anxiety to God. Then He spoke to me and said "I am saving the best till last." But that might not mean me. With two minutes to go I wondered if my slot had arrived, but someone else stood up to give a Bible reading and the pastor ended the testimony time. He looked at his watch then looked straight at me seated at the back. He said "We have run out of time, but I will let one more person stand and share." A quietness came over the church and not one of the two hundred and fifty people there moved. I briefly paused then moved to the front. I told the story of Les, his back, the drink, his hand, his life, the bitter and sour whisky. It was the long version as above, that you have already read.

At the end the congregation were out of their seats, cheering and clapping for God. Then I told them about yesterday and the lady with the leaflet, how I didn't know I was in the same place till I walked in, how I had waited during the testimony time, how God had talked about saving the best till last, not meaning me, but the story and how it could encourage them, about the pastor looking at me and wanting one more person and you know what? God cannot be beaten.

The people seemed so happy to hear the story that I had tears of joy running down my face. The pastor led the people in

My Walk With Jesus

cheering and clapping for God. At the end people came with prayer requests, as they had the previous night. They all knew that the results came from God, and all I could do was petition Him.

Back at Mum's I told her all that had happened and how amazed I was before finally calming down.

Eve Came Round For Prayer

Finally at home, later that day my sister Eve, married to Mike, rang to apologise for not being at the Saturday night prayer meeting but that she had heard all about it and how people had been encouraged. She went on to say that she felt that she should come over for prayer.

We prayed about various areas of her life. My hand was on her head, but suddenly it started to shake and I could not stop it. I felt the rushing of the Holy Spirit and said that to Eve. Suddenly she passed out and fell to the floor where she was under for some minutes. An amazing feeling and an amazing day.

The rest of the story concerning Eve is hers and hers alone. We cannot intrude past this point.

Dear Reader, I challenge you today to become obedient to God and follow the path that he lays out for you. An awful lot of the time I do not have a clue what God wants next. Sometimes one follows a gut feeling, that could be a hunch, could be the Holy Spirit, could be one's conscience and one goes along with it in faith. Only you know if it is from God or not. He might have to repeat Himself or someone might back it up or God might speak. God chooses different ways to make us understand.

"And Jesus looking upon them said, With men it is impossible, but not with God: for with God all things are possible."
- Mark 10:27 KJV.

As God is all-powerful He desires that we walk in the shelter that He provides. Sometimes when we act in faith the outcome is not what we expected, but that is not our concern. God sees the big picture and only He knows best. Our concern is continuing obedience to He who created the universe.

"Trust in God with all your heart, and do not be excited by your wisdom. In all your ways make wisdom known, that it may make straight your ways, and your foot will not stumble."

- Proverbs 3:5-6 LXX.

A Prayer

- Have mercy, O Lord, on all who travel, and save all those who are sent on duty: our fathers, mothers, brothers, sisters and children, all our loved ones and all Christians.

Eve Rang Me About Testimony Time

My sister Eve rang to ask if I was coming up to Mum's for the weekend. Apparently a new place of worship had opened and all the other places were going to visit. They were having a testimony night on Friday and Eve thought that I should go. This was another prompt that I should be sharing these stories that you are now reading. As it was one hundred and sixty miles away it would appear that I was not allowed to offer distance to avoid the responsibility.

At midday on Friday I started the journey and arrived in good time for the meeting that night. Eve and Mike were present to greet me amongst around five hundred people. Lots of people stood up to share things, but once again I felt that there was not really any display of God's power or even of an example of direction leading to an opportunity of God's work. It made me humble to realise that such extraordinary things had become almost a matter of routine in my life. Surely this should be normal for all Christians? I knew that I had to speak, but people were being called by name and no-one up front knew me. I mentioned this in a quick prayer. There was a woman minister who welcomed all the different groups and asked everyone to stand and pray for all of the visitors. Randomly I prayed for the man in front of me who then span around and gave me a big hug and asked where I was from. I replied that I was from far away Weston-Super-Mare and would like to give a testimony. He took me by the hand and led me to the front and gave me a microphone. The woman minister seemed uneasy with this stranger and what he might say. She brushed my shoulder and told me to hurry up. It was 22:30 and perhaps she wanted to call it a night and dismiss everyone for home.

They Do Not Accept Testimony

Though I talked fast I did not allow a time limit on what I was saying as it was about God. She kept on interrupting me to say that time was running out and to wrap it up before I was finished. I felt like I was being publicly embarrassed for talking about God's deeds. However after the event a number of people came up to ask to hear the end of the testimony.

An elder of the place led me outside and told me to leave to which I asked if it would be alright to return on Sunday and perhaps recount another of God's events. He informed me that I would not be coming back.

Later brother-in-law Mike said that it was the wrong time to give that testimony, but I didn't understand as I thought that I had been prepared for it over the course of the week. Why should people not want to hear about God's work during a specific evening for relating such incidents? The fact was that some people are simply not believers in the same way.

There is One, Holy, Universal, and Apostolic Church set up by God. And there are lots of groups set up by people who want to be the pastor, who have no theological training, no ordination but a strong sense of their own entitlement to lead.

Addressing Doubt

The next day, Saturday, found me up early and in deep thought about the events of the previous evening. I was confident that God thought it about time that my testimonies were shared and there had been plenty of recent opportunities that backed that up. Eve phoning me for an evening of supposed sharing counted as such an opportunity. The fact that I would be driving that one hundred and sixty miles anyway to be on their doorstep was not a coincidence when God is involved. But the reaction from the hosts was so negative that I was put on my guard and so I needed to ask God that the initial instruction to share was correct. In the end whatever happens with my own little life is not my concern, what is my concern is that I do God's will and seek to live by His guidance and direction and use the gifts and blessings that He has bestowed, in accordance with faith in Him.

My prayer to God was that He confirm to me whether my sharing the previous evening was of Him or me pushing against the flow. I turned Mum's TV to the God channel as it occurred to me that someone on there might be talking about these matters.

Prayers Are Confirmed On God TV

The previous evening I had talked about the incident in the bungalow when there had been a strong smell of flowers despite there being no flowers in the house (page 17), the voice telling me that I need Jesus, the argument with my ex and my foolish breaking my own hand, of being alone and eating beans on bread: all leading up to my giving my life to God. I had also gone on to tell of my selling the house and living on the kindness of friends and acquaintances for a year. Yes it was a long testimony, but all the parts were important as they all pointed to God.

So, sitting in Mum's lounge I put on the TV and the first words I heard from the man on screen were "Do you remember when you sold your house for me?" My mouth fell open and I actually answered the TV saying "Yes I do." The man on TV said "Do you remember being alone in your lounge and eating bread and beans?" "Yes, I do!" He said:

> "A person's steps are directed by the Lord,
> and his way by will."
> > - Psalms 36:23 LXX.

And with that the channel shut off.

That seemed like the pretty specific confirmation that I needed. My desire is to walk with the Lord and it looked like God was outlining this new task. Immediately I rang Eve and Mike and they were thrilled that I had not been set back, and that I had been given new resolve. Ask, seek, knock.

> "Ask, and it shall be given you; seek, and you shall find; knock, and it shall be opened unto you: For every one that asks receives; and he that seeks finds; and to him that knocks it shall be opened."
> > - Matthew 7:7-8 KJV.

Computer For Rachel

Rachel was twelve and required a computer for school work. I knew nothing about computers except that they were expensive, so I kept my eyes open for a second-hand one.

That weekend Rachel and I again went to see my Mum. On the way we stopped off to see my brother Terry who had a business selling photocopying machines. He mentioned that he had a five year old computer for sale for which he wanted £400. I did not know if it was a good price or not but Rachel wanted it so I bought it.

Months later Rachel's knowledge of computers had grown and so she asked for a newer model, more up to date. I inherited the old one and braced myself for a visit to a computer shop. Rachel found the one that she needed. The old one stayed in my back room as everyone I knew refused it.

At work John the fork-lift driver said that he wanted a computer, so I brought in mine. He returned it the next day complaining that he tried to update Windows 95 to Windows 2000 but it had crashed. I took it to Graham in my worship group who worked with computers and two days later I called to collect it. On the way I was praying that God would open new doors in my life without being really specific, whatever He does I will do my best to rise to the challenge. God knows best.

The computer appeared fine, but then Graham said "How do you feel about a blind date?" I was floored. I didn't know that Graham and I were that close, plus I had been single for eight years and certainly not thought about women ever since, enjoying the single life. However had I not, just a few minutes before, been asking God to open new doors? I could not say no to a new door, but have to let the path unfold as God directed. I said OK to Graham and he told me about this woman, and set up a time and place. Graham and his wife came to break the ice. Graham's description had led me to a mental image of the woman in question.

On A Blind Date Met My Future Wife

We met all of us in the pub. We men were on time and waiting patiently for the ladies to appear. As I waited for my blind date a summer breeze of loveliness floated through the door. She was beyond my dreams, beautiful and I knew that she was beyond my reach but how strange that I should be attracted by this vision whilst waiting for my blind date. Well, you have guessed it, she was indeed my blind date. I wondered if it were possible that someone so fantastic could be the new door I was seeking. Simply trust in God, I told myself, and He will let me know the path that I am to take.

At the end of the evening I asked to see her again and she allowed it. Graham and his wife arranged the next date at their house for a meal. There was a football match on the telly and Graham thought that we might all enjoy watching it after the meal. We did not know that Jan was anti-football so she didn't turn up and we instead enjoyed the food.

The third time was the following night when we went to the Pavilion pub. Jan said that she had upcoming major surgery but was trusting in Jesus to bring her through. Due in Bristol hospital the next week I enquired if she needed a lift and she said no thank you, she had one. Bearing in mind that if this was the sort of door that God wanted to open in my life, then I had better be ready, it would have to be me that took her in.

The night before she went in on Monday she rang to ask if the offer was still on as her lift had fallen through. She was in hospital for two weeks and the surgery went well, though she was frail and weak and needed looking after. Every evening I visited but Jan was mostly asleep. One evening we went for a slow stroll down the corridor and Jan said "Now you have seen the worst of me, it can only get better."

It was a three month recovery period at home, not allowed to return to work in the hair salon, still with stomach pains from the surgery, and the painkillers did not seem to offer much relief.

Prayer For Jan

Eight weeks after hospital and there seemed to be no improvement so I asked if she had prayed for the pain to stop, she hadn't, so I offered. I went onto my knees in front of her in the chair and asked Jesus to take away the pain from the stomach. On my next daily visit Jan said that the pain had subsided, but that there was still a dull ache. I prayed a second time that Christ would heal her. The next day she reported that the pain had gone. Jan was able to stop the painkillers and return to work after three months off. In that time it had been very special to me to be able to see her every day and she had also met my Mum and my family.

My sister Linda used to jest that I needed a girlfriend and I always replied that life with God is good. Linda said that she had various friends that she could introduce me to and I always replied that if God wanted it He would arrange it. Well God wanted, it was arranged and eleven months later we were married. It has been a long marriage filled with the sunshine of God's love as we are committed to each other and to Him.

Regarding a relationship with God, I have noticed that if you take Him seriously, He will take you seriously.

Brother Taken Ill And Flown To Miami

About a year and a half before meeting Jan my brother went on his twenty-fifth wedding anniversary to the island of Santa Lucia but whilst out there he was taken ill and flown to the nearest hospital, which was in Miami. Before they would do anything they took his American Express card and charged him $25,000 saying that he could claim it back against his insurance.

In the early hours of the morning my brother Terry's daughter Michelle rang with bad news, Terry was worse. Michelle was crying on the phone. I offered to come round to Mum's to comfort her. Whilst dressing I prayed the situation to God, that God would bless my path and for a safe one hundred and sixty mile journey.

Arriving at Mum's she gave me an update. It didn't seem to make much sense, but I continued to ask God into the matter. I rang the boss who kindly gave me as much time off work as I needed. For the next four days I fasted and read the Bible. I wanted to go and see my brother Terry, but it was a long and expensive trip and I knew that I would go if that was what God wanted. Fasting would clear the mind and concentrate the spirit.

My sister Linda rang and said that she was going to Miami and did I want to come with her. I said yes but that I needed to check that it was the right thing to do and would shortly ring her back. Seeking out a quiet corner I asked God what was the right thing for me to do. Staying in prayerful meditation for ten minutes the voice of God, eagerly awaited, spoke "I want you to go to Miami."

Next, on the phone to sister Linda I said it was time to book our flights, and we rang at the same time to try to obtain seats together. Just then Eve came round to see Mum and I informed them both that Linda and I were going out there and we would ring upon arrival.

When Linda and I landed there were police everywhere, which frightened us. A man had shot his wife. We arrived at the motel as quickly as possible, the same one that Terry's wife Bernie was staying at. She wasn't there, so we washed, changed and walked the short distance to the huge, maze-like hospital.

It took us a while to find Terry's room, but once there we could see that he was sitting up in bed chatting with Bernie, and really not looking too bad. He was pleased to see us and said that he would like to go home. But Linda and I know our brother and that you rarely receive the full picture from him. We consulted the doctor who said that Terry was quite unwell with a number of problems including a low blood count. We went back to sit with him and he let slip that he could hardly walk, that he was not eating and that his body was all bruised. When they airlifted him from Santa Lucia to Miami he nearly died and saw our Dad standing by his side, and that a priest had read the last rites. As Terry was not a Christian these things, especially about our deceased Dad must have struck him hard. At the end of visiting time he gave us money for food and we went back to the motel.

I said to Linda that I would be moving into the hospital room with Terry to help him, so she moved in with Bernie, saving the cost of one motel room. For the next four nights I stayed with Terry, sleeping on the chairs. Being there it was convenient to take him to the toilet or answer other needs. During the night the doctors took blood every hour on the hour – this was why Terry was black and blue. Terry could barely endure the doctors visits and implored me to send them away.

During the second night, about 2:00 AM Terry asked how I became a Christian. I wondered if this was the reason why I was here so I explained about the Gospel, about my own conversion story and how my life has subsequently been with Jesus and about some of the amazing things that I have seen. As I was telling Terry all this the phone rang and it was Linda.

Satanic Attack In Motel

Linda said "I don't want to stop here anymore. Bernie and I were having a glass of wine when the picture over the bed flew off and hit the bottom of the bed, then the two glasses of wine and the bottle went flying through the air, there was banging on the walls and the atmosphere turned bad." I suggested that she was the only non-believer in the group supporting Terry and therefore the weakest link. Satan is attacking because he does not want us here. Linda told me that when the banging on the walls was going on and on that she recalled that I had a small wooden cross in my bag, so she retrieved it and held it aloft and exactly at that moment the banging stopped.

The next morning the nurse came in with the newspapers as she had done the last few days, but this time instead of putting them on the bed she gave them to me and the top paper's headline was "God Wants Him Here For Freedom And God Will Deliver Him And Set Him Free." Certainly not a normal headline, judging by the previous few days reading.

Soon the doctor entered and said that Terry's blood count was up to normal and that he was free to go home.

Gift Of Two Seats On A Packed Plane

Terry and his wife immediately booked a flight back to Britain, but Linda and I still had a day to go till our flight. Terry wanted us on his flight, which would be an expensive change and it was Thanksgiving week, meaning that all planes everywhere were packed with families going back to see their parents. We were standing at the ticket booth in the busy airport trying to hear and being constantly jostled. Then God's heavenly voice spoke to me, clear despite the background hubbub "You will be on Terry's plane, but not sitting together." Less than one minute later the booking clerk called me over and said "You are very lucky, two spare seats have just come up, but not together." We boarded the aeroplane and from where I sat I could overhear a group behind me comparing notes on how busy was the airport and how packed the planes. Praise the Lord God for His amazing beneficence and condescension.

New Houses, New Occupiers

Returning to work after the trip and Terry's recovery it appeared that the building trade had hit a slow patch. This is the recurrent problem when self-employed, there is no security and when the contract ends, your income ends. However the big firm that I was with at that time managed to find me a little work on one of their remote sites. People were moving into the brand new houses that we had built, and that is a nice feeling as we finished off the other end of the estate. I enjoyed meeting the new couples. One elderly couple, Betty and Jack, were most welcoming and let me visit their house for breaks and eat my sandwiches with them. Jack's health was not good and he went to the doctor, who referred him to the hospital, and two days later he died.

To pay my respects to Jack and the family I attended the funeral and was asked to say a few words and a prayer. I was extremely honoured, being a relative stranger into their lives and being allowed to pay tribute to such a lovely man. There was a wake at the house.

The next day at work one of the bosses had a go at me. He felt that I didn't have to attend the funeral, he said that I knew that it was the Christmas rush and I had no respect for the company targets. This seemed wrong to me, surely people come first?

Jan And I Become Engaged

Some months later a Chinese family moved into one of the big five-bedroomed houses. As I came to know them they told me of their restaurant in town. I informed them that I would be becoming engaged later that year on Friday August 18th 2000. The two brothers offered to cater the evening function for us in their restaurant. On the day before the engagement I picked up the ring and popped into the restaurant to give it to them so they could help with the surprise.

On the evening I collected Jan, she was wearing a blue dress and looked stunning. In the restaurant I was the happiest and proudest man there. Before the starter arrived Jan was presented with a big bunch of roses and a bottle of champagne. So far so good.

Drinks were ordered and the starter of duck with wraps arrived. The little box that the wraps were in was opened revealing the ring. I thought "This is the moment." The restaurant was full, the table was perfect, Jan was beautiful and the ring was safely in sight. There are some important moments for any man and one of them is when he has to kneel and say "Will you marry me?" I took the ring and held her hand. People were looking. When Jan said yes everyone there roared and cheered and I slipped the ring onto her finger.

From that day we started planning the wedding for Saturday May 19th 2001. I realised that God had taken me a long way since those days of living out of a suitcase and moving from friend to friend.

Book Fell Off Book Shelf

Most nights I would ring my Mum, and we would discuss the family. That particular night we only talked about the weddings in the family. Jan and I invited all of my family, but my siblings were picking and choosing. I asked Mum if we should pick and choose but suddenly a book was pushed off the book shelf and landed open on the floor and it read:

"This festival is to be celebrated with all the family and to give glory to God."

I am becoming accustomed to God sometimes putting a sign in front of me that cannot be avoided as sometimes I am not sharp enough to spot the subtle signs. I told Mum what had happened and she was happy that the family would all be together.

Our Wedding

On May 18th, the night before the wedding, I slept at Les' house. I had chosen him as my best man. He awoke early and made a lovely big fry up for breakfast. At 7:30 we still had last minute preparations. I had gifts to take to the hotel where my family was staying and this was a good opportunity to see them before the wedding at 13:00.

The wedding was at Holy Trinity that we attended on a Sunday morning. I took my place at the front door to welcome the visitors, some of whom had travelled far. Jan's parents came over from New Zealand, a wonderful present of their company, considering the cost. For both of us this was a second marriage and Jan's Dad decided that he would not give her away and we respected that.

The time is now 12:50 and everyone is in, all smiling and cameras poised. I was standing at the front looking forward, as is the custom for the groom. I could hear the whispers that the bride had arrived. It was so tempting to look around, but I managed to keep my eyes to the front. Our wedding music started "From This Moment" by Shania Twain. When Jan was halfway down the aisle I was allowed to turn to look at her. I could not believe how beautiful she was, and she always has been in the decades ever since.

Jan's eldest son Martin gave her away and you could not envisage a prouder son. Her bridesmaids were her eldest daughter Carly and my own daughter Rachel, both looking lovely. As Jan closed in on me I was able to take her hand and express to her how beautiful she looked.

At the point wherein we exchanged vows and the rings, the sun appeared through a high window and a light beam shone right on us and we both agreed that it looked like a sign from God that He was happy for His children.

We were pronounced man and wife, we kissed and we turned to present the new union to our families. After the photos we arrived at the hotel for the meal, speeches, wine and the giving out of the gifts to the helpers who had made the day special.

The celebrations lasted all day into the evening, whereat more friends arrived to watch the first dance, to join in the disco and later the live music. Late at night Jan and I went for a walk on the sea front, she was still in her wedding dress and that is an image that will stay with me forever.

After the honeymoon we sold our respective houses and bought a property together in Banwell with three bedrooms and over time I put in a loft conversion.

Mum Moves In

After a blissful start to our marriage we had a phone call to tell us that Mum had had a fall. We rushed up to Mum's and a family meeting with the doctor who said that Mum needed to be looked after in a care home or with one of the family. The room fell quiet. Mum was looking pointedly at me, I looked at Jan and back to Mum. "You are coming home with us."

Jan was astonishing. She put herself into staying at home to look after Mum, handing in her notice at work and surviving on the small amount of Carers Allowance that the government awarded her. It was not easy, having to get up four to five times a night. But Mum was worth it, she loved being by the sea and we would take her out as much as possible.

One day Jan and I were about to take Mum for a doctor's appointment when she fell in the house and an ambulance was called; the paramedics confirmed a broken hip. After being released from hospital a nurse came twice a week to help Jan, but that used up the Carers Allowance. My contract was coming to an end and I was told that there was nothing available thereafter. No problem, I thought, let God know and He will provide. At break time I retreated to my car to think about matters and see if God was going to make me wait for this one. A text came through from a contractor offering work. Praise God, no waiting, no worrying. God is considerate.

Jan and I decided to move to somewhere closer to the new contract, but also more suitable for an invalid. The new place had a downstairs bathroom, but nevertheless caring for Mum became too difficult for us. Mum could barely walk and needed constant attention. We were sad when she moved to a residential home in Sandbay so we used to visit every day, the family would visit and we would take Mum for the weekend when possible.

Jan and I threw Mum an 80th birthday party and all the family came and Mum stayed the night. She loved that we were all there, as it was becoming rarer.

The Healing Of Vera

At the care home I used to sit and listen to other residents, they had had such interesting lives and could really tell good stories. Vera was telling me about her family, and as she did so it was clear that she was in pain. She already knew that I was a Christian so I offered to pray for her. Immediately after the prayer she said that she knew that God had healed her. The next day Vera called me over to say that her back was good. Thanks to our God, who created all and can heal all.

After only a short time in the residential home Mum was moved to a nursing home, and there she passed away at 82.

I continued to visit the residents, to give them a chance to talk and to talk about God with them. Three residents decided to become Christians. Jesus gave a parable about workers in a field who are all awarded the same rate of pay for their work, whether they worked the whole day or only the last hour. These three residents became Christians in their twilight, but they can still look ahead to the full hope of salvation like the rest of us.

Tom The Grave Digger

My friend Harry and I went to see Tom, 92, an ex-grave digger and each one dug by hand. He was not interested in God and his daughter Pat was concerned for him. She was a Christian and of course was worried about her father's fate in the afterlife. Pat asked us to pray for Tom.

The next week Harry and I once more visited Tom and listened to his stories and told some of our own about God's healing. This time Tom was interested and wanted to hear about the Gospel. He agreed with each point so we asked him what would stop him from becoming a Christian. Tom said that nothing would stop him, so we led him in a prayer of faith that Tom might start his Christian life.

Pat was amazed and could not believe it, she couldn't wait to see her Dad on his new path, but she did not press him on the matter as she wanted him to volunteer the information. She knew that he was stubborn and that if he had done this for real that he would be brimming over with excitement to tell her. She found him in his bedroom lying on his bed. He said "I am ready to die now. I have met Jesus and I am ready to go to God."

Two days later Tom passed away. That was leaving the matter of his eternal soul a bit late and Harry and I offered thanks to God that we could be used and that it had come to pass.

Work On The Doorstep

Monday on the building site and bad news, no more work. The building bubble of the early 2000's had come to an end and the whole trade had slowed. I had to go home. Whilst driving I passed the building site of another company and heard this Biblical quote:

> "A person's steps are directed by the Lord,
> and his way by will."
>
> — Psalms 36:23 LXX.

I went in and found the site manager who turned out to be with Bill, an old friend. I said that I was looking for carpentry work. Bill fielded the question, made a phone call and had me start on a site extremely close to home. God is amazing, His solutions are so complete and leave nothing unresolved.

Woman With A Puncture

That following weekend my daughter Rachel and I went for a drive in the countryside. Obviously trips to my Mum in Bedfordshire had now stopped. There was a car parked in a layby and a woman looking in her boot. The rain was coming in. I pulled over to help her. Rachel asked what I was doing and I said that I planned to offer help. The woman's first words were that she had just asked God for help and seconds later I appeared. We both agreed that providence is supple under God's guidance.

She had a puncture, but no jack. I had a jack but no puncture. My jack was for my model of car and might not fit any other, though of course it fitted hers. Soon her wheel was changed and she was on her way. Thanks be to God for allowing me to be the means of her help.

A Prayer

Glory be to the Father, and to the Son, and to the Holy Spirit;
Both now and forever, and unto the ages of ages. Amen.

Work Wife Tim

Tim was a carpenter that I had known for a couple of years. He rang when I was without work. He had a partner Rob who was off sick and I stood in for a while as they had a contract on a small site.

Come break times we would sit together and chat and eat. Tim was a very quiet Christian and did not always talk about God, unlike me. Also Tim did not seem to be living his faith, so I put two and two together and remembered that I had once been told that I encourage people. Perhaps my role here was to encourage Tim who was no longer even attending a place of worship. I broached the subject and Tim knew all that I had to say but didn't want to hear it, but each day he had an earful from me. My persistence was due to the feeling that God was using me so I had no need to worry about being seen as a nag.

The Healing Of Shaun And Jamie

You may paint your own mental picture about building sites and I am sure that one thing that you would agree with me is that talk about God is not normal, and news travels fast. Shaun the plumber came to see me. He had had a bad back and shoulder for a long time and he asked me to pray for him as he said that he wanted healing from God. Together Shaun and I prayed. Two days later and Shaun hasn't said anything about his back and shoulder, so I asked him.

Shaun said "I have been thinking about what you said about Jesus, and Him being the healer. My back and shoulder have been fine since the moment we prayed, but I wanted to wait and see if it was permanent." To demonstrate he flexed his back and shoulder in a free and easy manner. He continued "I have thought about this for two days and my conclusion is that I want to become a Christian. I want to live my life with Jesus."

When he said that his friend Jamie said "I do as well. I have been thinking about all those things that you said during break times; that Jesus is the only way to God and about my sins and about how Christ on the Cross takes away the sins of the world. Also, I have a bad back and want to be healed."

With Shaun standing on one side and Jamie on the other I put one hand on each of their shoulders and thanked God for each of them. Then I led them in a prayer for them to repeat and they started their new lives in Christ, new born babes in the faith.

> *"Jesus answered and said unto him, Verily, verily, I say unto you, Except a man be born again, he cannot see the kingdom of God."*
>
> - John 3:3 KJV.

Immediately after we had prayed Jamie said "My back has been healed." And we all praised God.

Shaun said "When I go home I am telling my Mum and girlfriend so that they can believe." I warned him "Don't bank on it." The next day he said that the warning was not without merit as neither of them believed him about the healing. I told him that when Jesus was here on earth that many did not believe Him and that they put Him to death. Even when they saw the constant miracles that Jesus performed day after to day to hundreds and thousands of people, a constant torrent of people, that the authorities still decided that persecuting Jesus was the right way to go.

> "If the world hate you, you know that it hated me before it hated you."
>> - John 15:18 KJV.

If we are to represent Christ on earth then we cannot afford to be offended in any way.

Eventually this little building site was completed and Tim and I moved to a site in Portishead. Work, but not good pay. As a believer I am happy that my future and destiny is in the hands of God and He will guide my steps.

> "A man's steps are directed by the Lord, and a mortal - how could he understand His ways?"
>> - Proverbs 20:24 LXX.

Ever since becoming a believer I have asked God for local work and God has always provided. By now Tim was growing in his new-found faith and each morning we would start the day in prayer then have a cup of tea. At morning break time we were having a sandwich together in the car when my phone rang. A contractor wanted Tim and I to work for him as soon as possible at a new site just minutes from where we both lived in Weston-Super-Mare. In fact Tim could see it from his house. The location was excellent, the pay was better than at present and even better it was for two years work.

Tim and I enjoyed that job, we were together and we both told all the other workers about God and His miracles. In the two years there twenty-three bosses came and went - that was certainly not normal. I like to think that as Tim and I were fixed for two years that the bosses were being circulated in and out so that they could hear something about God. I like to think that, I also know for a fact that life must be lived with both eyes fixed on God.

Tim's Panic Attack

After those two years we moved together to Long Ashton near Bristol. One morning Tim had a panic attack and went temporarily blind – there was blood covering the front of his eyeballs. I held his arm and led him into an empty house and laid my hands on him and prayed in the name of Jesus for the panic attack to stop and for his sight to be recovered. Immediately Tim recovered and the bright red blood across his eyes disappeared. Tim said that he had had this before sometimes and that the blood normally takes ages to disperse. He has had to constantly eat and drink coffee to calm down. To my knowledge Tim never had an attack again.

Avoid The A370

Jan and I were going to see her parents in New Zealand for her Dad's 80th and a big family party was planned.

The night before the flight I was returning from visiting my daughter Rachel but the motorway was shut and police were directing traffic into Bristol. I do not know the city at all so I rang Jan to say that I was going to be very late home due to being completely lost. As soon as I ended the call I started praying for directions and that someone would help me. Stopping at red traffic lights I saw a man in the car beside me who wound down his window and shouted "Are you OK?" I said that I was lost and needed to find the A370 to Weston-Super-Mare. He said "Follow me." I thanked God and breathed relief. The kind man had me on the A370 in a very short time and I was heading home.

Jan was surprised to see me so early and I told her the story. Jan's son Karl was there and said "That's not fair, you had God on your side." I replied that we can all be on God's side through faith and benefit from His guidance and direction.

In New Zealand Paul Prayed For My Back

The flight to New Zealand is long, tiring and complex involving buses, stopping in America for fuel before tackling the actual 24 hour flight, then another flight at the other end. After days of travel you can see why we always took a month when there to make it worth our time and the huge cost.

Jan's sister Paulette and her husband Paul lived there and took time to show us around the island. Paul would drive for the day then we would all stop at a motel.

During the second week I hurt my back, being in the back of a truck did not help. Arriving at the house as I climbed out my back went, my legs gave way, and I sat down in agony both simultaneously very hot and also shivering. I was asked if I wanted food but instead I crawled off to bed. Lying there seemed like a good opportunity to thank God for a good life so far.

Paul came into the room and asked if I would like prayer. Of course I said yes, and as he was praying I felt the Holy Spirit rushing through me from head to foot and straight away my back was totally healed. Big and constant thanks to God. We both went downstairs for food and the next day continued our adventures pain-free.

Ending a holiday like that is hard, tears flow at the goodbyes, the travel is awkward and tiring and in comparison Britain is cold and wet. Before long home life takes over and the holiday becomes a distant memory.

Whilst Thinking About My Mum I Had A Vision

On one particular cold and wet morning I was thinking about my Mum, the good times that we had had together, Rachel and my frequent visits and Mum and I talking and talking and talking. Suddenly my eyes filled with water and I saw a vision of a figure in a brilliant white robe coming towards me. I could not see the face, but as the robe became closer I could see that the chest part was open and there within was a rainbow of brilliant bright colours. I asked God what could it be and God replied that it was the robe of righteousness and the rainbow is the Holy Spirit. It was a powerful experience and as Jan slept upstairs I was in the kitchen sobbing.

Van "Heaven Here I Come"

That day Tim was off and as I drove to work a van cut in front of me with a sign on the back "Heaven here I come." I was thinking that I had never seen that van or that sticker before, and after the vision in the kitchen I was on the lookout for follow-ups. Thinking about all of these things made the day fly by.

A Dream About My Mum Walking Towards Me

That night I had a dream about Mum walking towards me. She was young, fit, smiling, beautiful and wearing lovely clothes. She was different, but still my Mum. Then three men approached me on horse back. I took this to be an emblem of God and I thanked God that He had seen fit to use me when Mum had become a Christian. The three men spoke together and said "That is what I have called you to do." I was moved by the dream.

Stopped On The M5 – A Boy Had Asked God For Help

The next day my boss rang and asked me to go to a new site for one day in Portishead. It was a nice day on site and a joy to meet new people. On the way home on the M5 there was a car on the hard shoulder. I wondered if I should stop and offer help but instead drove on. Although it is not legal to stop on the hard shoulder I could feel that I had done something wrong. I apologised to God and said that I would turn around at the next junction and go back to help them.

Exactly as I said that there was another car broken down in the distance. There were three boys walking in the field and another young man running along the hard shoulder carrying a petrol can - I stopped for him. He said "I have run out petrol and my friends have left me to walk home. As I was running I asked God for help and immediately you stopped for me." I thought about how God is amazing. My little lead up, spotting the four of them, deciding to offer help – all these things were taking place in good order for the answer to appear instantaneous.

As we drove to the petrol station he said that he was a Christian but his Dad was into black magic and would I pray for him? I did, and for the young lad too. We collected petrol and turned around at the junction to circle back to his car. I never saw him again but I reflected on this: that God is loving and true and sometimes He does not appear to answer requests in the way that we would expect, or even like. This may be on account of our lack of faith, or our impatience, or our demands that things are done our way. It is always exciting to me to step out of my comfort zone on God's behalf to see Him at work in unexpected ways and to broaden my understanding of Him.

Dear Reader, Jesus was walking on the water when Peter stepped out of his comfort zone to join his Lord on the water and walked out to meet him. Although Peter doubted when his intellect kicked in Jesus took his hand and together they reached the boat. Why not try stepping out of your comfort zone and walk with Jesus? He will be with you every step of the way.

Please understand that I am not saying that being a believer in Christ is easy. People may ridicule you, people are watching for you to make some sort of mistake and they are always willing to criticise and judge you.

Satan is one of God's fallen angels and he loves to trick and mislead humans, to make them ignore God. Please don't be deceived; God is real. Satan is a fallen angel because his pride said that he could take the place of God. Nowadays Satan tries to make us fall for the same error. He makes us feel proud of ourselves. It may be obvious pride over our appearance, but one of his specialities is to catch us with secondary pride. He may give us a temptation that is easy for us to ignore, and then we feel proud of ourselves. We think "How clever of me it was not to fall for that trap." And then BANG, we are caught in the sin of pride.

It may help to remember that Satan is a liar, a roarer, a slanderer, an accuser. He cannot read minds and he has no power other than suggestion.

However we humans have free will, an accessory fitted as standard by our Creator. If we were forced to love God we would be slaves. As we have a choice, choosing to believe in God and obey Him means that He treats us as His children.

Christ, one of the Holy Trinity, came to earth and joined Himself with humanity by being born of a human mother and her flesh and blood – Jesus. Later Jesus Christ was crucified and resurrected and so trampled down death by death, broke apart the gates of Hades, slew Hell and enabled the redivinisation of all reality. The death and resurrection of Christ becomes the gift that leads to salvation that is our hope for ourselves and our loved ones and all humankind, if we choose to ask for it and spend our lives in its pursuit.

"For God so loved the world, that He gave His only begotten Son, that whosoever believeth in Him should not perish, but have everlasting life." - John 3:16 KJV.

My Walk With Jesus

This also points out to us that Christ is not created, but is God. It is from here that the Nicene Creed (below) derives the word "begotten" meaning that Christ is derived without beginning from God the Father. However God created all things, including time. Therefore God is outside time, and so there cannot be a moment "before" the start of creation. Meaning that there cannot be a moment "before" Christ. The same is true of the Holy Spirit. He is not begotten of Christ, but of God the Father. So God the Father is the first person of the Holy Trinity, and Christ and the Holy Spirit are both different second persons, there is no third.

We humans are not begotten, we are born of a long line of other humans leading back to creation.

> *"Neither is there salvation in any other: for there is none other name under heaven given among men, whereby we must be saved."*
>
> - Acts 4:12 KJV.

This is the Nicene-Constantinopolitan Creed as set down by the Great Councils of the Church in 325 and 381 AD. It is the measure of any true Christian. That is, a true Christian states that they believe all the following. Those who subtract or add to it are outside the Church.

The Nicene Creed - The Symbol Of Faith

I believe in one God, Father Almighty, Maker of heaven and earth, and of all things visible and invisible.

And in one Lord Jesus Christ, the only begotten Son of God, begotten from the Father before all ages; Light from Light, true God from true God; begotten not made; consubstantial with the Father, through Him all things were made. For our sake and for our salvation He came down from Heaven, and was incarnate from the Holy Spirit and the Virgin Mary and became man. He was crucified for us under Pontius Pilate, and suffered and was buried. He rose again on the third day in accordance with the Scriptures, and ascended into Heaven, and is seated at the right hand of the Father. He is coming again in glory to judge the living and the dead. And His kingdom shall have no end.

And in the Holy Spirit, the Lord, the Giver of life; Who proceeds from the Father; Who together with Father and Son is worshipped and glorified; Who spoke through the prophets. In One, Holy, Universal, and Apostolic Church. I confess one baptism for the forgiveness of sins. I await the resurrection of the dead, And the life of the age to come. Amen.

As I continue my Christian life with God I hope that you are inspired, encouraged and motivated to start your own Christian journey.

Javid The Homeless

Christmas 2003. I was in town doing some shopping and sitting on the pavement was an Asian lad, homeless. I sat with him and we talked and made friends. I told him about Jesus on the basis that he would then have someone to ask who would certainly be able to help him with his problems in this world and the next. Then this poor lad named Javid said "I have two cream cakes, would you like one?" These two cakes were all that he had to eat. How is it that he who had nothing offered everything?

He started asking questions about Jesus and told me more about his lack of a home or income. He asked me to pray for him that God would provide help. Also he was on drugs.

We prayed together and we asked God for help for him. Sometimes God puts you in a position to help someone and you have the resources yourself to make a difference, but this was not one of those times. Any money that I gave, or accommodation, would go to feeding his drugs habit. Javid had to make the move himself towards God by really wanting to be free.

After prayer Javid said "I feel better, even though I have no physical reason for it." I said that I would come looking for him after Christmas. A week later I went back but could not find Javid.

The next day of work and a new labourer appeared on site named Andy. He joined us at break times for our discussions and he mentioned where he lived in Weston-Super-Mare. It was a house for the homeless that I had visited from time to time. I asked if he knew Javid. Andy said that he did as they used to live together in that house. He said that Javid used to be on drugs but now he seems to be clear of them and has taken up a job. I was thrilled at the news, but sadly it did not last as the drugs had a deep hold on him and pulled him back down.

A few weeks later I was in town on a Saturday and there was Javid. I went to be with him and to catch up. He said "I am waiting for the dealer to come along." I said that I had heard that he had been clean. "Why not walk away with me, give up the drugs before they kill you?" Before he answered the dealer drove up, Javid entered the car and they went off together.

Two days later Javid rang me and asked if the offer still stood. At that moment I was with Les and I told him the situation. Les said "Go and fetch him and bring him back here." We both went in the car to town and found Javid. He came with us and the next two weeks were up and down with the drugs. The third week I went to see Les and Javid who said "I want God. I want God. I can't take anymore, I need to change. Both of you, please pray for me." Straight away I went to my knees and I begged God to help him and fill him with the Holy Spirit.

After the prayer I pointed out that I had come straight from work and needed to go home, to wash and change and would be back in an hour. When I returned Javid was wobbling around like he was drunk. I asked what was going on and he said "I don't know, I can't stand up straight. It's a lovely feeling, I feel good." Les said that this started immediately after our prayer.

> "For these are not drunken, as you suppose, seeing it is but the third hour of the day. But this is that which was spoken by the prophet Joel; And it shall come to pass in the last days, says God, I will pour out of my Spirit upon all flesh: and your sons and your daughters shall prophesy, and your young men shall see visions, and your old men shall dream dreams."
> - Acts 2:15-17 KJV.

From that very day Javid did not touch heroin again and did not seem to go through cold turkey, but felt great. He started telling people about his new faith and what Jesus had done for him.

Prayer Time With Mike, Les And Javid
A few weeks later Javid was still living with Les. Our friend Mike went round to fix Les' TV. Before he left I asked if we could all pray together. We were all standing together in a circle with our arms across each other's shoulders and we prayed. Then Mike said that God had just told him something, but wouldn't say what it was as he wanted it confirmed through me first.

I shuddered as the Holy Spirit coursed through me and the words came tumbling out. Mike was saying "Yes, that is the message." Javid was crying because the message was a personal one for him.

As we disentangled ourselves Les let out a great shout "My hand, it's on fire. My hand is burning." He had never had this feeling before. I put it down to his proximity to the working of the power of God. The power that resurrects, the power that heals.

A month later Javid went back to the drugs, slipped out of the house and disappeared. Not every story has a happy ending, but it could have been.

A Dream About A Man Holding My Car
That night I had a dream that I was driving along Weston-Super-Mare sea front towards a certain house full of the homeless and all of their problems. The car was going very slow, it felt like something was holding it back. I stopped and walked round the back – there under the car was a man in black clothes and black hat holding onto the car. I made a grab for him and kicked him and he ran off.

Telling the dream to Les I said that I felt that I had to go to that house for the homeless. It was a job for me alone. I drove up to that house thinking that someone does not want me there. I had met most of the lads in there and had a little understanding of their problems and how they needed help.

Rob The Christian
Kevin had a room at the front but there was no reply to taps on the window and the room was in darkness. The room next door was lit up and there was someone standing at the window looking

into the darkness. He put out his head and asked if I needed help. I asked if Kevin was in, but apparently he was evicted for not paying his rent. He asked if I wanted to come in and opened the front door to me. We shook hands and he introduced himself as Rob and he told me his life story. He clearly had a void of love and care in his life so I turned the conversation to the spiritual. Before I left we had made friends and he had committed himself to a new life in Christ.

Tom The Christian

The next day I went again to see Rob and his friend Tim. Tim was a Christian who had lost his way and had a big drink problem. Another in the house, Tom, was into black magic and other harmful stuff. I felt that all needed refreshing about the love of God for them and His endless ability to help. Tim knew all this in his head but needed help putting it into practice.

Tom confessed that he wanted a change because only that day he had been drinking since breakfast and feeling terrible about himself. He went to the library and found books on black magic. He took these three books home, put them on the table and fell asleep in front of them. When he woke up the books had been replaced by three books on Jesus. He had no choice, he said, he had to read them. Tom wanted to know how the books could have been changed. I answered "God is easily capable of miracles. In the Gospels He turned the water into wine; He can turn anything into anything else. Nothing is impossible for God."

Tom stood up and said "I am not happy with my life. I want to give it to God so that He can change it into something better." We prayed on the matter there and then. Tim was present and gave Tom a hug.

The next day I came back with a bag of clothes to share around. As I walked up to the house Tim was looking out of the window, he saw me and smiled and shouted "I don't believe it." He said that he been thinking about how they needed help and God had sent me to them. "After you prayed last night I slept like a baby and this morning didn't want any alcohol, whereas I normally drink from dawn to dusk. I simply had breakfast. I want to praise God."

Rob, Tom And Tim Give Their Testimonies

Tom and Rob walked in and wanted to know what time was church in the morning. I said that I would pick all three of them up. The service included a testimony time and all three boys went up. It was very touching.

Timothy Has Cancer

Going back Tim said that he had bad news. The hospital told him that he had cancer of the stomach and not long to live. At the house I offered to pray for him.

The Healing Of Timothy

Tim was seated in a chair and I knelt down, grasped his hand and prayed. First I thanked God for Tim, praised God for always being so good towards us, for all the things that He has done in my life and continues to do, that I may become less that He may become greater, and that the cancer will go. I asked for the healing in the name of Jesus. As we prayed tears ran down Tim's face. We continued in prayer with me holding onto his hand whilst he moved around in his chair. When the prayer was over he looked at me and said "The pain has gone, I know that the cancer has gone. As you prayed a power ran through me and dissolved the pain. I know that the cancer has gone."

As we talked the new guy Kevin walked in, seated himself and listened to our conversation. Then he said "I give God everything." I said "Do you give God everything? God wants you, He wants to be in everything you do, He wants to be first in your life, He wants to be your first breath in the morning and to be thanked. He wants to be your last breath at night and thanked for the day. He wants to be in your heartbeat, to take away all fear. He wants you to follow Him, worship Him and live for Him." Before he could answer someone knocked on the door to offer Kevin some pizza.

Tim said "He never comes to see me and I have never heard him speak like that. Something is happening in this house."

Before I went home Tim wanted some prayer time during which he wanted prayer for all the people in the house. We prayed for all those with a drink problem, that it would stop, that the Holy Spirit would fill the house and touch every heart and change every one, and that all would see a change in these lads.

A Prayer

- Have mercy, O Lord, on our enemies: save all those who envy us, wish us evil or deal unjustly with us. May they not perish because of us sinners. Enlighten, Lord, with the truth of Your holy wisdom all who have gone astray from the Christian faith, led by destructive heresies, and unite them once more to Your Holy Universal and Apostolic Church.

Jacky And The Peaceful House

The next Saturday I arrived at 7:30 for breakfast with them all. At 8:30 the landlady Jacky arrived and as she walked through the front door we could hear her say "It feels peaceful in the house. There is a warmth and stillness about the place."

We were introduced and then she asked Tim and Rob what was going on. Why does it feel so peaceful and quiet? Tim said that it was God in the house and they now go to church. She was taken aback in a nice way and before she left she asked me to pray for her.

Around tea time that evening Rob said that there was a man upstairs who might want to go to church. He has seen a change in us and doesn't know how we are doing it and is praising us for coming off the drink. Rob ran upstairs to fetch him. We shook hands and he said something that encouraged me "You are different from the rest, you have something that most people do not have." And he asked for prayer. He was one of the few who are not outraged at the impertinence of gracious living.

Dear Reader, I know that God is alive and sees us and loves us and hears every prayer.

> "For it is written, As I live, said the Lord, every knee shall bow to Me, and every tongue shall confess to God. So then every one of us shall give account of himself to God."
>
> - Romans 14:11-12 KJV.

Many people do not believe in God, but that does not affect the fact that God exists. According to the philosopher-scientist Karl Popper it is not possible to prove a negative (that something does not exist); it is only to prove something positive (that something does exist).

> "The fool said in his heart, 'There is no God.'"
> - Psalms 13:1 LXX.

To know absolutely everything is a skill only possessed by one person – God. How much knowledge is there to know out of everything that exists in the universe? Well, obviously 100%. How much of that is known on earth? In your town? In your life? We can quickly work out that of all the knowledge that exists, what each one of us knows is less than 1% - we can't do the maths to work out that the actual figure is much smaller. If each of us knows such a small part of all that there is to know, from where comes the confidence to claim with authority that God does not exist?

How does anyone know that God exists? By meeting Him and seeing the powerful things that He does. Having seen cancers healed in several people, Les' back healing and all those hard-working labourers healed, can anyone shake me of my confidence in God with mere clever words? No. Experience beats reason.

John Broke Down In Car And Prayed

The next day at work John the labourer came to find me. He wanted my reaction to something that happened to him over the weekend. John said "I drive an old car that keeps breaking down and it broke down again. For some reason I thought of you and what would you do. So I asked God for help. Suddenly three men appeared and pushed the car to the next filling station and put in some petrol then they disappeared. The car then worked. What do you make of that?"

I answered that John knew what I would say, that you asked God for help and He did. What else could you expect? John said "I don't know. I am fed up of this car and this job – please pray that I will find a new job."

John Has A New Job

A week later the site manager offered John a new job as his assistant, with a car. John came to me "I don't believe it." "You better believe it, John, God is already involved in your life." In due course John was made site manager in his own right on another site.

It is amazing how God places other people around you ready to help. Try genuinely asking for help and see what happens.

Tim Had A Dream

The building trade was up and down during the 2000's and it was a constant problem trying to keep in work. Tim and I talked about what a relief it would be to exit the building trade. On the way to work Tim shared with me a dream from the previous night. He was on his mountain bike and finding it hard to keep up with the bike ahead. He could not see the rider's face, but could see that he was on a racing bike and had all the correct bicycling gear and helmet on and was gliding along without effort. Tim looked down at the speedometer and saw that he was doing 50 mph. Then he woke up.

Tim asked me if I knew what it meant or could interpret it. I paused in prayer for a minute waiting for God to provide the answer, not me. "Tim, the meaning is this. The man on the two bikes is you. At the moment you are finding it hard to keep up, but you will keep up. You must continue to grow stronger in faith, not trusting in yourself, only in God. You will change from the man on the mountain bike to the man on the racing bike prepared with all the right kit. You are finding it hard to keep up at the moment, but you saw that you were doing 50 mph so you will make the change when you are fifty years old." At the time he was forty-eight.

The two years flew by. He took to listening to the Bible on an MP3 player and we spent time praying together. This was good for both of us. Tim became more involved at our place of worship and wrote and played worship songs in the band.

Our work time together lasted a good five years and it was great encouragement for both of us. The building trade was still bad but we still did not have any ideas for a change.

Tim came to me in work and said "I had another dream last night. What do you make of this? I was in the back of our bosses

Transit van. Rod was driving but did not look around. In the back of the van there was all sorts of building material such as glue and screws and nails. Rod took me on a journey but I didn't know where. Then I woke up. What do you think?"

Again I paused to push myself out of the way to allow God clear space to work. "The meaning of the dream is this. Over all the time we have worked for Rod we have been provided for our material needs through the work and you see that all around you in the van. But now it is time to move on, because the faceless man that you saw in the driving seat was God and He is going to take you on a journey. But you are alone in the van, I will not be with you. You will be working with your hands and some building materials and God will continue to provide for you, as always."

Some months later that site at Long Ashton came to an end and we were moved to Portishead. It was slow going and the site was full of carpenters, and we could see that this was going to be our last site. Just before we finished Tim had a third and final dream. "I was working then I put down my tools by a long window and walked away. What do you make of that?"

Once more I paused to offer a little prayer that God would take it from here. "Your site work is coming to an end. You will rid yourself of your tools or even sell them. Leaving your tools by a long window indicates that God is giving you the light of understanding over your new path. This is a new door in your life and you will not have to look very far. God will make it quite visible for you."

The site completed one week later giving us an opportunity to wait for the Lord to provide our permanent jobs. For a short while our friends kept us busy with home improvements. The last job that Tim and I worked on together was some painting. During this Tim told me about an interview for a caretaker in a school where Tim knew the headmaster. He was offered the job. There was indeed plenty of light shining on his path as things were simple and obvious. Tim did sell most of his tools as he no longer needed them. Praises to God from us both.

Shortly after that it was my turn and I received a job working for a company with three care homes. This meant that I could sit with residents and listen to their life stories. Many were excellent stories.

One Saturday morning Jan and I went to visit a lady in one

home who was a devoted Christian and also one hundred today. She showed me her card from the Queen with a bright smile that lit up the room. I asked if I might pray for her. At this her face shone as she took my hand and closed her eyes. I am glad that she did as I had tears flowing down my face. What a moment and what an opportunity to spend that time with her and with the Lord. She knew that her time on earth was drawing to a close and that she looked to Jesus for salvation and to be with her as she crossed into eternity.

The Move To Kings Lynn

Time moves on. I continue on my walk with Jesus. Jan and I continue trusting in God for direction and opportunities for obedience. Work is still up and down and I am working part-time and Jan's hours are dropping, so we thank God for giving us funds aforetime and put our house on the market.

Now, in the past such moves have always been in response to a prompt from God, but now no such prompt has been provided. However Jan and I felt that there was no point in sitting on a house worth a lot and asking God for more, and also that the change would do us good.

We sold with some speed, but took a while to find anything to buy in our price range. Jan has horses so we also need a bit of land and some stables. We looked around Devon and Wales and noticed a house in Norfolk that met all of our requirements.

Jan and I had a long discussion about it especially the location so far from my daughter Rachel and Jan's eldest son Martin, but decided that we would take it. Rachel had been having something of a bad year: her flat was broken into, the flat upstairs had a burst pipe and flooded her place; then problems at work sparking her departure and search for another job.

It was nearly time for our move and I prayed that Rachel would be offered a permanent job before we moved. And in fact it was the day that we moved, as we were driving to Norfolk that Rachel rang to report having been offered a job in the NHS call centre.

The new house required a lot of modernisation and updating – a lot of which I could undertake myself, but the materials and parts were still expensive. Jan and I did the work together and to this day I maintain that it was Jan's painting skills that transformed the house into our home.

A Job With The YMCA

Living on the difference between the house prices enabled us to put in nine months work on the new property and then we needed to find work. Jan had worked as a hairdresser for most of her life, and me on building sites and we felt the need to branch out. It was not an easy new life, we both lost our cars due to malfunction or rear-end crashes. Jan found work first in a pub. She did not enjoy it, but the money helped. Then I was interviewed by the YMCA to work with youngsters aged between sixteen to twenty-one on Saturdays and Sundays, then supporting them through the week if they needed help with skills such as listening, encouragement, guidance, cooking etc.

I felt that the job was right for me and praised God for giving it to me, even though they didn't tell me that I had the job for another two days.

Norfolk did not suit me and Jan knew it, life was difficult and Jan took on a second job as a hairdresser. She cut her hand at work that became infected and so required surgery and a two week stay at Norwich hospital. That entailed a one hundred mile a day journey for me to see her.

Because of all this I had to struggle to remind myself that we were trying to follow God's will and that life is about other people. It's not about where or what I want, it's about being where God wants.

Eventually Jan was ready for work but decided not to return to the salon or the pub, opting for a job in a care home. She had done this many years ago and enjoyed it. I was still part-time at the YMCA but had that feeling that it would not last.

Joe The Christian

One of the young men came to me to hear about Jesus and after a few weeks he said that he understood the complete message and wanted to start his own Christian life. He attended a local place of worship and became baptised and gave his testimony.

Joe Has A Dream

Weeks later Joe had a dream of a little boy scratching at the Bible. He asked me what I thought about it. I replied "When a dog is a young puppy it feeds from its mother and is constantly looking for food. You are that puppy, young as a Christian and seeking wisdom and knowledge. As you become experienced in spiritual matters you will find that God is easily able to provide for all your needs."

> *"Man shall not live by bread alone, but by every word that proceeds out of the mouth of God."*
>
> - Matthew 4:4 KJV.

> *"Each day feed yourself on God and read the Bible and you will grow."*

Gary The Christian

Weeks later a new lad came to live in the YMCA house. He loved football and his knowledge was encyclopaedic. He would talk for hours and when I came on shift he would pounce and ask me football related questions.

From time to time the conversation would turn to spiritual things and I took the opportunity to probe Gary on his belief in God. He did not want to know. I said to him "If you ask God to show Himself, he will." The next time I was on shift Gary was totally different. He said that he had followed my suggestion and that it had worked. As a consequence Gary felt that he had no choice but to pray to God and ask Him into his life, and that after this he felt that he was now a part of something bigger and eternal and born into a new life.

We both had big smiles and I asked him to tell me more. Gary said "Well, that night I was thinking about what you said and before going to bed I prayed to ask God to show that He is real. I had this dream: I was on a journey through space and darkness toward the moon. Then I turned around back to the earth. As I closed in my life flashed before me, but the earth refused me and I could not land. I was frightened and it seemed to me that no one would offer help. Then suddenly the earth became God. It was powerful and changed me but I still don't know what it means."

As before I let God take charge and the meaning presented itself. "Gary, this is the meaning of the dream. God gave you a dream of the past, the present and the future. The journey through space represents your life of rejection and no light to aid you on your way or any escape. You were heading towards the moon, but the moon does not produce true light, it is only reflected. You were going in the wrong direction. You turned around when you heard about God and your life changed to a better course. People often say that when you die your life flashes before your eyes. When this happened to you, you were about to die, not physically, but to your old spiritual ways and become reborn as a child of God. When this happens you cannot make friends with the world, so you could not land. You were frightened because you wanted to exit the darkness and be truly accepted. As the earth transfigured to be God you realised that the earth and everything on it belongs to God, that God is in control and is calling you and God is sending you the message 'When you have nothing in this world and all you have left is God, then you have everything.'"

It transpired that a couple of weeks ago Gary had been homeless and had been rejected by his family and this had caused him much pain and many tears.

Dear Reader, God, in all His grace and mercy, waits patiently for you to call out to Him. For many people this is when they are at their lowest point. Remember my own story about being brought to my knees? (Page 78). That was ten years ago. I was a broken man with nothing left and no where to go. But not all of us need to wait till our lowest point. God's love is constant and accessible each day. He wants each of us to turn to Him.

Keither The Christian

The YMCA had several hostels and I worked in all of them, meaning that I came to know all the residents, male and female. After one resident found that I was a Christian it would not be long before they all knew. One lad approached me and asked my views on dreams. I answered that usually they are just dreams, but from time to time one sticks and you feel that there is a message in it. I went on to give a couple of examples of my own.

"One morning I was in bed and God woke me up with a loud message saying 'Roy, preach the Gospel.' I jumped out of bed saying 'Yes, Lord, where do You want me to go? Into town?' I made a cup of tea and as the kettle was boiling the front door bell rang and there were a pair of Jehovah's Witnesses[4].

> *"But though we, or an angel from heaven, preach any other gospel unto you than that which we have preached unto you, let him be accursed. As we said before, so say I now again, If any man preach any other gospel unto you than that you have received, let him be accursed."*
>
> - Galatians 1:8-9 KJV.

"God woke me up that morning to do something for Him. So yes, I believe that we should examine the dreams that seem important."

I told Keither the following story.

"Whilst working at the YMCA I had an interview with another hostel and was accepted. They showed me round and introduced me to the staff but I could not start until the CRB[5] was clear. I waited months for some word from the company that they had had it, but no word, and it was wearing my patience thin. I contacted them and they said that my references had still not come back, so they could apply for the CRB. This seemed odd, but I continued waiting. They even asked me to go on a two day course. Then it was six months after the interview. I was still part-time with the YMCA but still waiting for a permanent job.

"At home the heavenly voice, strong and clear said 'You do not have that job.' For a moment I was confused, because the manager had said that the job was mine, and I had been on that course. When Jan came home I told her what had happened. We agreed that listening to God was more important than that job and we had best ignore it.

"Soon it was nine months with no proper work and much to my relief the YMCA offered me a permanent post. It was on contract so meant more security. And that is why I am here today."

Keither then recounted his recurring dream. Each night a big, black wolf sits and stares at him and then pounces on him. I asked if we could pray about it to ask God for release from this

---

4   Jehovah's Witnesses are not Christians. They say that they have Christ, but a created one. Therefore they revile Christ.
5   Criminal Records Bureau. A police check on any criminal activity.

nightmare.

The next morning Keither told me that that he had had a dream about a wolf, but it only stayed seated at a distance and looked at him. We prayed again, and that was the last time the dream occurred. Moved as a result of this intervention the following evening Keither gave his life to God as we prayed together and afterwards he said that he felt a total release as if a heavy weight were lifted from him, and in consideration of his sins he felt the forgiveness that God had given to him.

Stacey The Christian

Shortly thereafter his girlfriend Stacey was moved by the change in Keither, started to attend church and in a short time started her own Christian life.

James The Christian

Not long after these events the hostel played host to James who saw what was happening with the other young folk, and he felt that such a dedication to God would improve his life. He said "My life is a mess, I want to change." So we prayed together and he joined the ranks of those on their brand-new Christian journeys. During the prayer his face was glowing red and at the end he said that he was very hot and said "That feels lovely, like I have just climbed out of a hot bath and I feel totally clean from inside out."

Dear Reader, even when one is a believer life goes on and there are difficult times. One by one only the Christian lads were evicted from the hostel and some months later I was suspended for talking about the Gospel – in a Christian hostel. Three weeks later the charges were dropped and I returned to work thinking "God will not be out-done."

When things start to go wrong, and they will, simply trust in God, hold onto your faith and stand firm. God is doing a good work through you. The comfortable will be discomforted as God seeks the best through us all. In calmness, serve Him.

"For I am not ashamed of the gospel of Christ: for it is the power of God unto salvation to every one that believes."
- Romans 1:16 KJV.

Mike The Christian And The Wild Deer

Some time after these events another lad arrived at the hostel who said "I've heard good reports about you." We retired to my office for a cup of tea and to hear about his situation and requirements. He wanted to hear about the religion that the other boys were taking up and especially about Jesus. I shared a number of testimonies with him. After an hour of these Mike said that he would be coming back with his girlfriend to hear more.

The next evening they came round wanting to hear more testimonies and listened to them until 22:00 at night. Mike then had to take his girlfriend home but promised to resume the conversation upon his return.

On his way home Mike took a short cut through the cemetery and in the distance he saw a wild deer. He looked into the sky and prayed "God, give me a sign that You are there. If You are real let me go and stroke that wild deer." The deer turned to look at him and seated itself. Mike went to it and stroked it for some time before returning to the hostel. He was very excited and came to tell me all that had happened. For him this was sufficient proof of God's existence.

As we talked Mike noticed a Bible on the shelf and asked to borrow it. I said that it was a present for him to keep. Right away he opened it and at the back of this one was a model prayer for those who wish to give themselves to God. Mike started to read it out loud and as he was doing so he said "Wow, I can feel a sensation going right through me from head to foot. Can you feel anything?" I said that no, I couldn't. He continued to read the prayer out loud and said that the sensation was increasing. God seems to know how to reach people according to their individual needs.

Leaving The YMCA, Then It Changes Hands

A short while later I said to Jan that I felt that my time at the hostel was coming to an end and a week later I was offered a job in Kings Lynn at a care home. The timing was great as shortly thereafter the hostel was sold on. However I felt that my time there had been worthwhile; working with the homeless, preparing them for life in the outside world and independent living and most of all seeing the change inside them with those who had come to know God.

Lower Farm Care Home – A Tree Across The Road

We are now up to Monday October 28th 2013 and I am working at Lower Farm Care Home. For the past night there had been storms over Norfolk with high winds and torrential rain. Leaving home twenty minutes early because of the weather. The radio said that trees were falling and it would be best to stay home. I am quite stubborn and wanted to go to work, but through all this the best I could manage was twenty miles per hour, the windscreen wipers swinging like the clappers and the high wind tried to lift the car.

Usually the commute to work each morning is a great time to indulge in prayer for the family and other matters that spring to mind. This time I was going slow and keeping my eyes glued to the road. All of a sudden a car appeared from behind with his lights on full beam sitting an inch off my back bumper. As I turned a corner I was confronted by a tree lying across the road. I stamped on the brakes and shut my eyes. This caused the car behind to nearly crash into my rear.

What happened next is beyond my explanation, and I can only lay the miracle before God as it underlines the fact that He can do anything. As the car behind slammed me into the tree I felt briefly myself go into a bubble that seemed outside of normal time and events. I soon exited it and opened my eyes to see what was going on. I found myself on the other side of the tree still driving up the road. When I checked the rear view mirror I could see that the car behind was stopped on the other side of the tree trunk, the driver was standing on the road looking at me driving away. I often wonder what he saw and thought.

Wales

A year later Jan and I decided to move again to find more land for the horses, and decided on Carmarthenshire in Wales. A bungalow with land, three stables and a horse tack room became available.

Believing that where we live is where God wants us I kept asking for updates on the directions until they appeared. God has known what we would be like before we were born, everything about us.

As with the previous move the bungalow required quite a bit of work and as I was unemployed I was put to work at home. We gratefully found grants that would help modernise the house and prevent heat loss.

Jan On Her Horse

After two weeks of solid labour Jan thought it would be good to take the horses out for a ride. She saddled up and I followed behind on my push-bike to make sure that she was safe. We turned off our drive onto the main road that is signposted forty mph, but the traffic usually goes much faster. On the return journey a car was right behind me revving his engine and he overtook at great speed, but as he did so there was a great bang, as if he had hit something. Similar to the previous story about the tree on the road I was once more in a bubble and I could not see out or indeed anything in the bubble, including me. I did not feel worried about the bang.

After a brief pause I came out of the bubble of protection and the first thing that I could see was my right hand on the bike, then the back of the car, then Jan on the horse that was jittering all over the place. Jan was shouting "Roy, are you alright?" and I replied that I was fine and we kept on going. At home Jan examined my arm whilst I told her what had happened. Like me she accepted that it was divine intervention. I have no idea why God keeps doing amazing things and protecting me, but I can tell you that I am deeply grateful.

About a month later I was offered a job with a maintenance company. The work was OK, but there was a lot of travelling and late hours and many hours spent on the motorway. Although grateful for having a job I knew of a care home ten minutes from home so popped in there to see if they needed anyone in maintenance. They didn't but three months later rang back to say that they would like to offer a full-time job and that they had a couple more homes in the area and that I would be splitting my work between them, as required. That day at work in my current job I was called into the manager's office so that he could lay me off as the company was closing down. He must have wondered why I was smiling.

The Wrong Post Code

My new boss Julie asked me to deliver something for her. She had had a locksmith out to her house and needed to pay him. My sat nav took me to a country lane with two houses. I knocked on both, but no reply. I wondered what to do. Why did I wonder? I knew exactly what to do, I prayed. God has never let me down. At that moment a police car appeared and drove straight to me and asked if I required assistance. I showed him the post code and he said he knew the area and that I was fifteen minutes away. He directed me through as many lefts and rights as I could retain, then said I would have to ask the rest of the way. Exhausting the directions remembered I arrived at another place in the middle of nowhere so again I asked God and stopped at a junction.

A woman driver turned in behind me. A minute later the heaven-sent voice said "Follow the woman behind you." I wondered how I could follow when I was in front and the road was narrow. Turning a corner there was a woman walking her dog so I stopped quickly to allow the car behind to pass and to ask more directions to that post code. She said something amazing "I don't know, but you should follow that car in front, she knows where it is." I set off after the car and when she stopped I told her the whole story. She said that she knew where the post code is, "It is that house right there."

God is amazing and will never let you down.

Keeping A Diary For Twenty-Five Years

As I said right at the start in the Foreword, very early on I felt that God wanted me to write all this down. As the years unfolded I kept an A4 lever Arch file to which I regularly added more pages in my scrawly handwriting as the miracles occurred. The file grew large and cumbersome until, about twenty-five years from the start God told me it was time to stop. Looking back on the miracles it was clear that the bulk happened whilst in construction, and the second batch at the YMCA.

The notes were kept as a diary as I had no notion that they would ever be seen by anyone else. But soon after I was told to stop I received a message that these hand-written notes should be published. Published? That was way beyond my experience. How on earth to go about this? I had absolutely no idea. This was in mid 2019.

Whilst working at the care home nearest to my own house I saw a man in the main corridor and I started to tell him my story and my thoughts concerning my twenty-five years of notes concerning my walk with Jesus. At that point I didn't even know his name; upon reflection I have no idea why I was even telling him about the notes and the new imperative to put it into print. I went on with my worries that I knew nothing about publication or even how to transfer the notes into a useable format. Where would I find someone to help me?

He smiled and said, "That's what I do." He went on "Yes – and I will do all that for you."

Wow! Thank You, God.

You will have noticed, as you travelled on my journey with me, God puts people in place sometimes before we even know the question to ask. It is clear to me and to my family and friends that God arranged everything, my career changing over the years to end up in a care home ten minutes from my house, and the reasons that are personal to himself why that man was there that day. In fact I later found that he had been there one day a week for nine years waiting for "the missing Christian". That is part of his story, not mine.

God had his own plan from the day He told me to "Write it all down" right up until I needed my writing proofread and published. And now here you are, holding my story in your hand. God is AMAZING.

Epilogue

Well, that's my book. You have met me and you have met my family. You have seen me at my lows and at my highs and in my normal working life. You have read of my mistakes and those times when God has used this uneducated man as a channel for the work of the Almighty.

There is simply too much other stuff that I should have said. There should be a lot more about reliance on the Church, the Bride Of Christ. We Christians are all part of that body, I am only a little toe and cannot be part of the work of God unless part of the Church. I am sorry that it was beyond my scope to also include more of this, as it is through the Church that God gives us support, strength and it is there that we can call upon for wisdom and guidance. All spiritual matters should be under the watchful eye of a spiritual father or director.

There are times in this book that I have tried, in my small way, to describe some important points of theology. Really this is best left to better minds than mine. All I want to do is outline my God, the Creator of all, the Trinity, the joining of Christ with humanity, and the sacrifice that enables all of us to ask for, and live in the hope of salvation. A trained theologian could have done a decent job.

All I am is a carpenter and my speciality is to be part of a team that builds houses - I have helped to build thousands of houses. In the course of my life I have met and valued thousands of interesting people. All of them needed God's power and help in their lives. If I have gifts, they are to encourage people and to see how God can be applied to their problems of health, addiction, emotion, relationships. All of those people struggling to find an answer, and there is only one answer: God.

All of the stories above that you have been with me are absolutely true, every single word. Though the book has passed through an editor for help with the language and spelling I have insisted many times that the stories themselves remain as they happened. These stories have been a part of my life and parts of the lives of so many others. I give them to you now for two reasons; to encourage those whose faith needs a jolt, to remind you that God is huge, powerful, loving and can be turned to for every single thing in your life. Also these stories are for those who are not sure, or who do not believe. It will not benefit me if you turn to God and start your very own Christian life full of the miracles that will happen around you. I will never meet you, I will never receive money or preference for your turning to God. Only you will see the difference, and what a difference you will see.

I feel like a man who has discovered that eating fruit is better than eating mud. All I can do is go around in my excitement and say to people "Try it! Try it! It's brilliant, it's amazing." God is amazing.

"O taste and see that the Lord is good."
- Psalms 33:9 LXX.

For now my journey must come to a close, but it's like everything in life - all will come to an end. They say life begins at forty, but I was nearly forty when my world fell apart. Your life has it's own ups and downs, but with Jesus in your life you will have direction, peace, joy and hope for the future. As I look back to the start of my Christian walk with Jesus, I learned to trust in Him and that He will do the rest. You will see what an amazing journey God will take you on.

Each one of us as a story to tell, whether it be someone else's life, or your own. Take hold of your life and don't waste it, don't count the days but make them count. Each and everyone of us has a window of time and our days are numbered. Each one of us is only one final heart beat away from eternity. Then what?

The meaning of life is in Jesus and nowhere else. Challenge yourself to open up your heart today, right now and start your own walk with Jesus.

Editor's Notes

Normally the editors is a silent voice. It is my job to type up the notes that Roy has collected over twenty-five or more years, to correct the grammar and syntax and tighten the story-telling somewhat and other miscellaneous tasks as well as finally pushing the book through the publication process. However Roy has asked that I relate to you my take on all the above.

I am an Orthodox Christian of 54 years, hence a lot longer than Roy and of a totally different and considerably older way of doing Christianity than the novel Evangelicals. However Roy's book has changed my life. I recognise his fervour for Christ, and his totally strange way of praying.

It has been my long practice to present to God other people in prayer, some of whom have temporary problems which require attention, but only the big problems for myself. I did not want to burden God with my petty little problems, broken cars, etc etc and was wary of the Biblical warning to not tempt God.

Roy's stories tell of a different approach, he offers every single detail of his day to God and asks Him about every little thing. Noting the wonderful results that God has provided in answer to those prayers it seemed to me that Roy was saying that to NOT give every detail to God was to tempt Him, and that a complete life in Christ means giving up every last semblance of control. So you know what, why not try it? So I did, one day, during normal morning prayers I went through the packed day ahead of me that seemed like there would be overlapping appointments and use of a vehicle that was regularly breaking down. I gave each item to God and then watched the day.

Normally everything goes wrong for me, but on that day in the evening I retreated to think about what had happened. Each appointment was met, had time lavishly poured upon it, and even though several were many miles apart the vehicle held together and did not break down. I tried to count up each little "good luck" moment of the day realising that they were blessings in return for the trust placed in God, and there were too many to count. This must have been one of my best days ever.

It has only been a month since trying to adopt this new way of thinking but I can also vouch that it has brought me great peace of heart to feel that I may relax into life; and wherever I am it is because that is where I am required to be. Roy has used the word "amazed" a lot. Now I understand why.

- Editor. August 2020.

"Hold nothing back from God."
                                    - Roy Smart.

My Walk With Jesus

Printed in Great Britain
by Amazon